I0569599

A PLACE CALLED THERE

A MEMOIR

GIA L. JAMES

© 2024 by Gia L. James. All rights reserved.

No part of this publication may be reproduced, distributed, or transmitted in any form or by any means, including photocopying, recording, or other electronic or mechanical methods, without the prior written permission of the publisher, except in the case of brief quotations embodied in critical reviews and specific other noncommercial uses permitted by copyright law.

This book may reference third-party trademarks, service marks, and products as a convenience to the reader. These references are not intended to imply endorsement of or affiliation with any company or product. Trademarks, service marks, and product names are the property of their respective owners.

First Edition

ISBN - Paperback: 979-8-9907817-0-2 /Hardcover: 979-8-9907817-1-9

Printed in the United States of America

Published by ShevMar, LLC

www.giajames.com

CONTENTS

AUTHOR'S NOTE

This story is a truthful recounting of my life and experiences, presented as accurately as my memory and the accounts from family members allow. To respect privacy, I have changed or excluded the names of specific individuals. The dialogues and exchanges within these pages are not verbatim but are crafted to convey the essence and impact of these moments faithfully.

DEDICATION

For my loves, Andy, Jazmyne, Jordyne, and my little dog Teddy, who faithfully sat at my feet as I documented my journey.

To the two women who contributed to my very being: my nature mother, the late Patricia Ann Blackston, and my nurture mother, Myrtle Ball Garrison.

One gave me up for the other to lift me up and give me the life I was born to live.

FOREWORD

My wife's life has many chapters I have been blessed to share as a friend, lover, husband, father, and soulmate, starting with the first chapter as ambitious and invincible students in the Summer of 1983. What is chronicled in the pages of this book are the chapters of her life that culminate with the miraculous union with her four biological brothers and sisters after her remarkable and incredible pursuit to address the curiosities and questions as an adopted baby that also came to life with the birth of our second daughter in 1995.

The book has something for everyone, whether you are a biological or adopted child, a biological or adoptive parent, or had the privilege of having an adopted person in your life.

Be prepared to cry, laugh, and be inspired by Gia's story of perseverance and its indelible impact on you.

Best regards,
    Andrew S. James

INTRODUCTION

Born in the vibrant heart of New Orleans and raised under the expansive skies of Houston, Texas, my life's flavors have always hinted at a deeper story waiting to be uncovered. Despite my early relocation, a mysterious bond with New Orleans' rich culinary traditions remained, whispering tales of a heritage I yearned to explore. My journey has been a voyage across continents, through the tapestry of human connection, and most profoundly, into the essence of my identity.

For adoptees like myself, embarking on a journey of self-discovery to uncover our origins is a deeply personal endeavor that touches the core of our being. If you have ever pondered the roots of your existence, I hope my story serves as a beacon, guiding you toward discovering that missing piece in your life's puzzle. Venturing into the unknown to find my biological family was daunting, yet it unfolded as one of my life's most exhilarating and fulfilling chapters. This story chronicles the fears and triumphs of that journey and celebrates the profound connections and revelations that come with finding where we truly belong.

Through the narrative of finding my biological family, which proved to be one of my life's scariest but BEST and most rewarding experiences, I aspire to inspire you to embrace the pursuit of your origins, should you long to do so. It's a path fraught with uncertainties but rich with the potential for unparalleled joy and a deeper understanding of self. My story, a testament to resilience, humor in the face of adversity, and the profound belief that everything happens for a reason, invites you on a journey of discovery, connection, and the endless quest for 'A Place Called There.'

CHAPTER 1
SURVIVAL MODE

The night that nearly ended my life is as vivid in my memory as if it were yesterday, a stark reminder of how quickly everything can change. It began abruptly, with a desperate struggle for air in the stillness of the night, a battle that grew increasingly frantic with each failed attempt to breathe. The more I struggled, the more my anxiety soared, creating a vicious cycle of fear that threatened to overwhelm me.

Despite not being alone in my home, the fact that my family was nearby, yet oblivious to my distress as I recuperated from a recent surgery, somehow intensified my panic, pushing me towards an automatic fight-or-flight response. In that moment of heightened alertness, I realized something was profoundly wrong, something out of the ordinary that demanded immediate and decisive action.

Asthma or any form of respiratory illness had never been a part of my life; there was no inhaler within reach, no oxygen tank on standby to alleviate the suffocating fear. My search for answers led me to a familiar yet unexpected place: a bookshelf in my home library. There, amidst a collection of mundane literature, sat the "Complete Guide to Symptoms, Illness & Surgery" by H. Winter Griffith, M.D. It was an odd companion for a partially ambulatory mother, awakened by a dire need for air, yet there I was, thumbing through its pages in desperation.

The house was silent as I was separated from my daughters and my mother-in-law due to a renovation project that had disrupted our usual familial proximity. My husband, Andy, half a world away in Sweden, was unreachable, leaving me to face this ordeal armed with nothing but a medical reference book and a fierce will to survive.

As I rifled through the pages, seeking a clue, a diagnosis, anything that could explain the tightness gripping my chest, I found myself in the section on breathing difficulties. The symptoms on page thirty-nine mirrored my experience, a discovery that was both a relief and a new source of dread.

"Sudden breathing difficulty. Sharp chest pain that worsens with inhalation." The description matched my symptoms precisely, except for the growing anxiety that seemed to feed the cycle of fear and make each breath a battle. Sitting up brought a slight reprieve, suggesting that whatever was afflicting me might be manageable, at least temporarily. Yet, disturbing the rest of my household felt unnecessary, a decision I might regret if the situation worsened.

But as I delved further into the possible causes of my symptoms, the words "Blood clot in the lung. Collapsed lung" leaped off the page, etching themselves into my memory. The advice to seek immediate medical attention for something as serious as pulmonary embolism was a wake-up call, not just about my health but about the very foundation of my identity.

Until that night, my approach to medical history had always been somewhat cavalier, a joke about being "potluck" due to my adopted status. But faced with the genuine possibility of a life-threatening condition, the gaps in my knowledge about my biological heritage suddenly became a chasm too vast to ignore. It was a realization that set me on a path of discovery, not just for my sake but for the future of my daughters, Jordyne and Jazmyne.

The journey to uncover my biological roots was daunting, filled with unknowns and the fear of what I might find. Yet, the need to know became an urgent quest for truth to fill the gaps in my medical history and understand the genetic legacy I might pass on to my children. It was a search that extended far beyond the pages of any book, beyond the confines of my home, reaching into the past I never dared to explore.

As I reflect on that night, the fear, the desperation, and the eventual resolve to seek out my origins, I am reminded of the profound impact that moment had on my life. It was the beginning of a journey that would take me from the uncertainty of my health crisis to a discovery of a family I had never known and a sense of identity that had always eluded me.

Born on October 2, 1965, in New Orleans, Louisiana, and adopted by Myrtle and Isaac Peter Garrison, III, shortly after, my adoption was never hidden. They named me Gia Lana Garrison. It was a fact of my existence, as natural as the air I breathed, yet it was an incomplete story, a narrative waiting to be entirely told. Growing up, I never felt out of place in my family; I was loved, cherished, and celebrated as the "Chosen One," a special designation that filled me with a sense of belonging and pride.

My family never treated me differently than any other family member. I grew up feeling special because my parents knew they wanted a little girl. I believed they went to a store and chose me as their bright, shiny new object they desired, instead of being born to them. To better understand, here's a little background about the family who adopted me.

My adoptive family's history, from my nurturing mother Myrtle, who came from a humble background in Texas to the complexities of their marital struggles, framed my early years. Myrtle's resilience and independence, particularly in facing my father's challenges, set a powerful example for me.

My mother, Myrtle, is one of five children born to Frances and Pat Ball, Sr., with one of her siblings being a fraternal twin sister, Mildred. My mother also has two other sisters, Pauline, the oldest, and Margie Nell, the youngest. They had one brother, Pat Ball, Jr., or "Sonny Boy," as he was referred to, who was the oldest of all the siblings. The Ball family children were all born in Beaumont, Texas, but their family migrated to Galveston, Texas, because of my grandfather's occupation. There, my mother and her siblings attended Central High School. They grew up poor but claimed they never felt it, nor were they ever hungry. All five of them had to share things like all their toys, including only one bicycle, but through her upbringing, I can see how my mother became such a nurturer in her own right.

Myrtle and my Aunt Mildred graduated from Central

High in 1954. They both decided to attend Prairie View A&M University, where they majored in Nursing.

After graduation, my mother was employed for two years at the University of Texas Medical Branch in Galveston as an Operating Room Nurse. She wanted to become a Nurse Anesthetist, so in 1960, she enrolled at the Flint Goodridge Hospital School of Anesthesia. After she completed school, my mother stayed in New Orleans, working at the hospital where she met her husband and my father, Isaac Peter Garrison, III, or "Pete," to his friends and family.

Pete was a native of New Orleans and worked as a Business Manager for the same hospital. Like my mother and aunt, he also attended an HBCU or Historically Black College or University. Pete graduated and attended Southern University to become a Certified Public Accountant later. Before they married on July 8, 1961, in Galveston, Texas, Myrtle lived at a nurse's residence on the grounds while Pete resided with his parents.

After marrying, my parents moved to Colosseum Street in New Orleans. Due to infertility issues, they decided to start their family through adoption.

It was in 1963 when they adopted their first child, a son about thirteen months old. According to my parents, my brother was considered a challenging placement and had been moved several times between different foster families before finding his home with our parents.

Unfortunately, after his adoption was finalized, my parents started having marital problems. I later discovered it was primarily due to my father's struggles with alcoholism and his mismanagement of the couple's community funds. From what I understand, Myrtle wanted to try to save the marriage; however, Pete refused to go to marriage counseling. Like many Black men, mainly born in the same era, Pete looked at counseling as a form of weakness, so Myrtle went alone, intending to save their marriage.

Despite all this, Myrtle longed to have a daughter to add to their family, but she was afraid that if she divorced Pete, she would not be granted her wish. My mother knew that, at the time, the agency would not place children in families that were having marital discord. Therefore, Myrtle and Pete signed a petition from the Children's Bureau of New Orleans to adopt a girl.

In early 1966, the couple was informed that a girl was available. They placed me in the home temporarily to ensure that the union would work out for a trial period of approximately six months. The agency continued monitoring the family during this time to ensure the environment was stable. Upon completing the six-month trial, Myrtle and Pete agreed to keep me, and I was placed permanently through a closed adoption. The new birth certificate was granted, thus erasing who I was at the time of my birth. With a new name given to me by my adoptive parents, everything was finalized. As far as any of us were concerned, that was all I would ever need to know.

My parents decided to purchase a newer home with more space to accommodate their growing family and perhaps their increasing conflict, so they relocated us to Lafaye Street. The Lafaye Street home is the earliest recollection of a home I can remember. The floor plan was a ranch-style, three-bedroom, two-bath home, and it was located one over from the corner house. I also recall that the corner house had Great Dane dogs as pets, and when we walked down the street, I'd feel tiny, especially compared to them.

My mother continued to work and would leave us in the care of the Hospital nursery childcare program located on the hospital grounds. This was primarily for her convenience, although my father continued to work in the same capacity. This was likely due to Myrtle moving through life, functioning in ways similar to that of a single mother, as Pete's drinking and money mismanagement continued to spiral out of control, as was the case throughout a good portion of their eight-year marriage.

In 1968, Myrtle requested a legal separation and successfully gained permission from the court to take the children and leave the State of Louisiana. I was three years old, and my brother was five. After leaving Pete, my mother decided to relocate back to Texas. She thought there were more hospitals, meaning more work opportunities and a better family support system.

As luck would have it, Myrtle noticed a desirable job listing in a Houston newspaper while quietly planning her move. Knowing she would be the primary parent financially responsible for my brother and me, she completed the application, got her anesthesia license reciprocated by the state of Texas, and began working three days after relocating to the area at MD Anderson Cancer and Research Hospital in the Texas Medical Center.

At first, we lived with Aunt Mildred and her husband, Uncle Billy, and their family for a few months until Mom could purchase her own home. It would take her a few months of working and saving, but when she could, she bought a single-family ranch-style home in the Brentwood neighborhood of Houston on Beran Street. It was a three-bedroom, two-bath home where one of the rooms was all my own. Our house was across the street from James Madison High School, with Aunt Mildred and her family living only ten minutes away in the Windsor Village neighborhood in the southeast section of Houston.

Although our family was split, my father sent apologetic letters begging my mother for forgiveness and to return. Nonetheless, their divorce was finalized in 1970, and my mom was granted full custody of me and my brother. My father was ordered to pay seventy-six dollars per child each month in child support, but he failed to comply with the decree.

The court also granted Dad visitation rights during the summers for several weeks, during which he exercised his rights to remain in our lives, or so that's what he wanted my mother to believe.

During this era, when airports didn't have security checkpoints, and families could meet loved ones at their gates or see them off, my brother and I would fly to New Orleans as "unaccompanied minors." This is where the airline would be responsible for getting us from gate to gate and, essentially, from parent to parent. My memories of those times start off like those of many who visit New Orleans, spending time in the French Quarter. I was about five or six years old, and my father would frequent bars there. My brother and I would be set up outside the bar, sitting on the corner where we'd spend time people-watching as my dad was set up inside the bar, drinking the day away. He checked on us occasionally, bringing us cherry colas and snacks to soothe us as we waited for him to finish, which sometimes took hours. All I knew was that if my mother ever found out, there'd be hell to pay.

After a while, Dad lost the Lafaye Street home and waffled between couch surfing and homelessness. Eventually, the house was auctioned off with all of its contents. Mom stopped our visits because of Dad's instability, lack of housing, and his lack of interest in seeing my brother and me. Despite all his pleading before the divorce, once she made this particular decision, he never asked to see us again. When I was seven, Dad came to Houston to take me and my brother to Astroworld for the day. That is the last time I saw him as my father.

After relocating to Houston, our lives took on a new rhythm, distinctly marked by my mother's determination to provide for us. Our home on Beran Street symbolized new beginnings, where I could carve out my space, literally and figuratively. The proximity to family provided a sense of community and support that had been missing in New Orleans, reinforcing the values of love and resilience that would guide me through the challenges.

As the narrative of my life unfolds, this chapter serves as the foundation for a journey of self-discovery and identity. From the night of my health scare to the exploration of my origins, each step has been a move toward understanding, acceptance, and a deeper connection to the past. My story is one of overcoming, bridging the gap between the known and the unknown, and ultimately, finding a place where I truly belong.

"For I know the plans I have for you, declares the Lord, plans to prosper you and not to harm you, plans to give you hope and a future." - Jeremiah 29:11

CHAPTER 2
FAMILY MATTERS

My brother and I navigated our childhood with a resilient and joyous bond, facing life's hurdles with unwavering support for one another. Our life, filled with happiness and contentment, was shaped by moments that, though simple, were profoundly significant.

One unforgettable memory occurred when I was just a toddler, wandering out of our home late at night in search of our mother, who was away due to her demanding job. This episode, a testament to the challenges of single parenthood, underscored our mother's sacrifices, working on-call hours to secure our well-being. It was a night that showcased not only my vulnerability but also the community's kindness, as a stranger and the local police ensured my safe return to my mother's arms.

Most of my memories come later in life, like when we moved in with my Aunt Mildred. I was only about three.

As we settled into life with Aunt Mildred, these early experiences underlined the importance of family support and the deep bonds we shared. It was a time of adjustment and growth, enriched by the closeness we found within our extended family.

In 1973, my mother started working as a Certified Registered Nurse Anesthetist with the Houston Anesthesiologist at St. Luke's and Texas Children's Hospital in the Texas Medical Center.

We had lived with my aunt until my mom could afford to buy a house, and it was the first house I had ever lived in with just my mom and my brother. I don't know why I remember, but the house cost $17,000. After she purchased it, they told my brother and me to sit in a specific spot inside the empty house while they walked around to check it out. It was ranch-style with three bedrooms, two full baths, and a two-car garage. She raised me there through high school.

Although she was now officially a single mother, my Aunt Mildred was like a second mother. Through the years, I've always felt a sense of closeness with Aunt Mildred's family and her children, my cousins. Their proximity to our house, less than ten minutes away, made this bond even tighter.

We also had a close bond with my Aunt Margie and her husband, Uncle Felix, who lived in Colorado, where my brother and I would spend the summer. A few of my fondest memories of that time were playing with my cousin's hamsters, going fishing in a small lake for these tiny little fish that we actually scaled and fried up later, and having pancake-making contests to see who could make a giant pancake without it breaking apart while flipping it.

The adventures that followed, especially our summer in Colorado, were filled with joy and laughter. From camping in the Rocky Mountains to the unforgettable trip to the Sand Dunes, these experiences brought us closer to nature and each other. The incident at the dunes, where I stubbornly wore shorts against the elements, remains a cherished family tale emblematic of my youthful determination and the warmth of family ties.

I was a tiny little thing, yet I was one to stand firm on whatever I made my mind up to do. Well, one day, they told us we would see the dunes, and I needed to change out of my shorts, which I did not want to do. I insisted on wearing those shorts, and once we were there and the storm picked up, I soon realized why I needed to have on pants. Fortunately, my older cousin, Denice, wore bell-bottom style pants, and I had her stand behind me so I could wrap the edge of her pants around my skinny, exposed legs. The memory of us just laughing with her and me huddled together with all that sand blowing around us still tickles us when we reminisce down memory lane.

While my mother continued to work as a CRNA, it was also important to her that I attended private school. Mom usually worked the seven to three shift, so I would have to wake up early at five o'clock so she could get to work by seven. That is probably why I'm not a morning person. Although school didn't start until eight o'clock, I had to get up at five, get ready, go with Mom to work at seven, and then I would leave her job's parking lot to walk to my bus stop in the Medical Center, which was like a 15-minute city bus ride away from St. Vincent's.

My first school experience was at an Episcopal school named St. Stephen's. The entrance exam I took before being accepted consisted of matching various colors and shapes, and I must have passed with flying colors because I was a student before long. There, I thrived, also participating in the Brownies until the fourth grade.

My secondary school was a Catholic School named St.

Vincent's de Paul, which I attended from the fifth through eighth grades. Mom kept me active by enrolling in extracurricular activities such as swimming, gymnastics, tennis, and art lessons at the Jewish Community Center. I also took ice skating lessons at the Galleria for many years and reached an intermediate level as a figure skater. I remember taking lessons from Mrs. Tinker, my piano teacher. She taught me from elementary school through junior high.

Once I graduated from St. Vincent's, I attended an all-girl Sacred Heart school in the Memorial section of Houston named Duchesne Academy of the Sacred Heart. This was a very different experience for me as it was not co-ed. It was also different due to some life lessons learned while attending Duchesne Academy.

Duchesne was very far away from home. Mom continued to wake me up at five o'clock every morning so she could arrive at work on time for her shift. On the way in, Mom would drop me off at the school bus stop near Rice University in the Village section of Houston, adjacent to the Houston Medical Center, so she could get to work on time before changing into her scrubs for the day. I would then go into a nearby office building where I could see the bus stop and stay warm until it arrived.

As I was waiting, more students would come, so I was rarely alone. We had to ride for about one hour each day to get to school, picking up more students living in Houston's River Oaks section along this bus route.

I remember River Oaks was "untouchable" for people who looked like me. It had a reputation for privilege and exclusivity. However, the reality was I could attend the same school as they did, even coming from "the other side of the tracks," as our assumed wealth appeared to vary despite my mother owning our home and cycling through new vehicles. Yet this behavior wasn't a surprise as I spent my whole high school career at Duchesne, where there were only seven Black girls in my graduating class. This was also the largest population of Black girls to come through one class at Duchesne that we knew of then.

Several instances of prejudice occurred along the way, but being the naïve, sheltered little girl I was, I did not view it as such at the time. The cases occurred since I had not been exposed, making them unidentifiable.

One experience, however, was life-changing.

When it was time to apply for colleges, students were assigned counselors to assist us. I remember going into the office and being coached on which schools I should apply to. When I would tell them which schools I wanted to attend, I was discouraged from applying there based on my average grades. Let me remind you that in Texas, there are a few rules and a heavy dose of school pride. So, being a Texas Aggie and attending Texas A&M University was my goal! I did also have some "reach" schools like Rice University and Carnegie Mellon University on my list, in addition to Texas Tech University and the University of Texas at Austin, just in case... but I'm rarely a second option taker as what I make my mind up to do it's considered done as far as I'm concerned.

When I went home and told my mother that I was discouraged from applying to my reach schools, she encouraged me to apply nevertheless because she believed I could get in. My mother felt that the counselors were dissuading me from applying there because they did not think that I, as a young Black girl, was worthy of attending such highly-rated schools. I remember the words Mom spoke to me like it was yesterday. These are words that I likely had no choice but to abide by, but that's another story. That evening, she looked at me and said, "Don't tell them you will apply. Just do it!"

Momma even went as far as to have a friend from school bring catalogs for schools she didn't plan to apply to, including Carnegie Mellon University. Schools my counselor didn't think I had any business applying to.

I got into every school where I applied except Rice University. I believe I did not get in because our class valedictorian's mother worked in Rice University's admission office. When I arrived for my interview and gave my name, she said, "Oh, you're Gia." I interviewed with one of the male admission officers, and I left feeling like it went well. Unfortunately, I did not get an invitation to attend Rice. Okay, transparency moment. I probably *didn't* get accepted to Rice because of the class valedictorian's mother, and to take ownership, my grades were just average. Of course, the class valedictorian got in.

However, everything happens for a reason. I got accepted to Carnegie Mellon University, the furthest school from Houston. After applying, my mother decided to take me to the campus in Pittsburgh, Pennsylvania, so I could get a tour to help me solidify my decision and go for my in-person interview. Yes, after. Before this visit, I had never stepped foot on their campus, so I had no idea what to expect.

When I showed up for my interview at CMU, I had no knowledge that I had already been accepted the day before! When we arrived, I recall a white male admissions officer who delivered the good news to my mother and me. He also attempted to discourage me from accepting the invitation by sharing every negative possible outcome that likely came to mind.

"It is too far away from home for you."

"You will get homesick, and it is freezing here in Pittsburgh compared to Houston."

"Coming up here would be like walking into a brick wall. Others who had a higher ability than you came here and failed, so they returned home."

If you come to understand anything at this point, it's that my mother is not one to coward to anything or anyone. Mom took me outside and assessed what she felt he was saying to me, again asking me to ignore it and showing that man what I am capable of was why I should go out of my comfort zone to attend CMU.

My educational journey was another area where my mother's influence was paramount. Her dedication was evident from the disciplined mornings that started before dawn to ensure I reached school on time to the diverse extracurricular activities that shaped my interests and skills. Each school, from St. Stephen's Episcopal to Duchesne Academy, offered unique challenges and learning experiences, contributing to my personal and academic growth.

The journey through these formative years was punctuated by prejudice and misunderstanding, particularly as I navigated the college application process. Yet, my mother's unwavering belief in my potential encouraged me to pursue my dreams, leading to my acceptance into Carnegie Mellon University—a decision that would shape my future.

I was also a student of many of her wise life lessons up until now.

I remember my mother wanting to buy me my first car. It was a cute little Volkswagen. It also had a manual transmission, and the dealership was straight across

Houston, outside of Katy. I wanted the car but didn't know how to drive a stick shift. My mother looked at the salesman and told him she would purchase it that evening if he could show me how to drive it home, which was precisely what he did.

Mom dropped me into both a lesson and test on the same day without me even knowing about it or prepping for it, but I'm so thankful she did because it further proved to me just how capable I am of doing anything I set my mind to.

Mom wanted me to commit to CMU, and they required a nonrefundable housing deposit of five hundred dollars to secure my spot. Mom decided we were not leaving Pittsburgh without writing the check to get the ball rolling. I could tell from the look in her eyes that it was essential to her for me to choose to go to CMU, and pleasing my mother was always what I strived for since she was always in my corner, so I acquiesced and said that I would go—giving up my dream to be a Texas Aggie, which was no longer my reality.

I later found out that my mother frequently heard the anesthesiologists she worked for and staff sharing updates on their kids, including places where they were accepted. According to the banter that often took place during surgeries, CMU is very difficult to get in, and by the tone of those around her, my chances of getting in were slim. Little did they know that I was my mother's child, and the day she would share the news of where I was going would turn a few heads.

Once I returned home to Houston and headed toward the end of my senior year of high school, everyone was gleefully reporting to the school counselor the schools they would be attending in the Fall. I held back my excitement from the counselor as long as I could until I disclosed my decision. As we were getting close to graduation, I was all too happy to report that I would attend Carnegie Mellon University. The look on my counselor's face was of the utmost surprise and total shock! It was almost hilarious to me. The ultimate satisfaction of defying and superseding any expectation while obliterating her limits for me was a very satisfying feeling.

Her half-assed congratulations utterances changed over to "Are you sure? Do you want to go so far away from home? Do you think you can keep up?" But what could she do then? Absolutely nothing.

Reflecting on these memories, it's clear that the tapestry of my childhood is woven with threads of adventure, learning, and profound familial love. My mother's sacrifices and support, the bond with my brother, and the shared experiences have indelibly shaped the person I am today.

"Don't be discouraged. It's often the last key in the bunch that opens the lock." – Unknown

---

CHAPTER 3
ONLY A MOTHER'S LOVE

While mom continued working and raising me and my brother, he started having behavioral issues in school. He was in the first or second grade at the time. With hopes of counteracting those issues, our whole family participated in psychiatric counseling. Mom also tried to put my brother in activities such as the Cub Scouts, Little League Baseball, football, and Big Brothers of America to give him access to positive role models and, hopefully, a father figure he could emulate.

Since we were members of the First Unitarian Church, we also did things with them, such as bike rides and visits to the park and the zoo. Sometimes, these activities would help my brother. However, sometimes, he would misbehave.

This continued to be a growing challenge, so my Mom had to find non-traditional learning environments for him to see where he would thrive. After several years of attempts and visits to psychiatric doctors, Mom enrolled him in Chinquapin, a boarding school, when he was in junior high.

Chinquapin's program was for boys with issues adjusting to a traditional school setting. It offered a college-bound program where students would reside during the week and come home on the weekends. As it was becoming more challenging for our mother to manage him, there were teachers at Chinquapin that she hoped could help.

After Chinquapin ended, Mom asked Aunt Margie, who was married and had two sons of her own, if my brother could stay with them to improve his situation further and his chances of succeeding in becoming a college-bound student. My brother attended the same high school as our cousins but did not traditionally complete his high school degree. Instead, he got his GED and joined the Air Force.

Following his service, my brother returned to Colorado, marking a new chapter in his life. When our mother visited him, she found him in casual attire, a departure from the military uniform she expected. They enjoyed a pleasant dinner together, focusing on their reunion rather than the details of his service discharge, which was honorably granted due to a mismatch with military training expectations.

Our family, including aunts, uncles, and cousins from various states, rallied around him, offering support and encouragement as he navigated his next steps. He tried living in Galveston, working multiple jobs, and even pursuing further education with our mother's and my support. Despite challenges, including some legal issues, our mother never wavered in her commitment, helping him enroll in a program to aid his transition into college and later into vocational training for a new career path.

His journey included moving back to Texas, where he faced and overcame various obstacles with our mother's unwavering support. She remained a constant source of encouragement, even assisting him financially and with personal needs when necessary.

Today, our mother continues to be a pillar of support, believing in the possibility of a brighter future. Our family's story is one of perseverance, hope, and the enduring strength of familial bonds.

This is one of the many reasons I know and believe she is a great, devoted, loving, and supportive mother.

"I have fought the good fight, I have finished the race, I have kept the faith." - 2 Timothy 4:7 (NIV)

CHAPTER 4
MY NEXT CHAPTERS

I graduated from Duchesne Academy in May of 1983, and I went to Pittsburgh that summer to participate in a program called the Carnegie Mellon Action Project (CMAP). This program was designed for students of color to come to the campus the summer before enrolling to give them a head start on the curriculum to boost us the first semester, so we had an advantage to keep the attrition rates lower.

During this program, I met other students of color from all over the United States. I also became familiar with the campus so it would be easier to navigate it come August, and I took a few science and math courses to get acclimated to college life. My first major was Chemical Engineering, which was most likely another reason I was admitted. Having Black female students enrolled in an engineering (STEM) program was highly sought after then, just as much as today.

I also met Andy that summer. Andy was in the Tepper School of Business Administration and an athlete on the Tartans varsity football team. One day, I was in the cafeteria. Andy had a work-study job, so he worked in the physical plant during the summer. I remember the first time I saw him, and he was very dark because he was outside working and digging in the sun all the time, making him sweaty. So, the day I met Andy, he was as dark as midnight, and I vividly remember it was a lovely sunny day.

He was eating with his friend Gene, who I was interested in at the time. Gene introduced me saying something to the effect of, "Oh, this is my friend Andy James."

I warmly said, "It's nice to meet you," but then returned my focus to Gene, whom I had eyes for. The three of us sat there and talked casually, and then it was time for everybody to get up and go. I was returning to my dorm room, and Andy mentioned he was going the same way as me, so he'd walk me there.

I remember the conversation. It was such an easy one. We strolled as we were getting to know each other, laughing with simple banter back and forth. This kept us together for another fifteen or twenty minutes.

I remember him dropping me off at the dorm and saying he'll see me around, and something in the pit of my stomach was like, wow! It stopped me, and I paused when I got to the door. I turned around and looked back, and Andy was standing there looking at me as I was looking at him. I couldn't focus on how or why, but that was the first time I started to feel attracted to him. It was just me and him, the ease of it all and the innocence of the conversation.

The rest of that summer, I would see him on and off just casually in passing. I still had eyes for Gene because he was all I could think about.

I'm not going to lie; I did get seriously homesick and cried endlessly, but eventually, I toughed it out.

So, there I was in a foreign place that summer, feeling homesick. The program had ended, leaving a three-week window between CMAP and the start of school. My mom had arranged for me to stay at a nearby college since I couldn't move into my dorm room on campus yet. Meanwhile, everybody else had gone home. Andy had also gone home.

I was in a strange city with no one to talk to. I didn't have anything to do all day except cry. It lasted about a week before I begged my mom to let me come home.

I flew home for the remainder of those two weeks and then returned at the onset of school. Being so far away from home was one of the reasons why I didn't want to go to school in Pennsylvania. I could never jump on a plane and head home whenever I felt like it. Until then, I had never really lived outside of Texas, which was also my home and where my family was, to go to a place I was not used to or the snow I knew would come.

I met my roommate during my first year. Her name was Marilyn, and she was from Altoona, Pennsylvania. I didn't know how she would take to me, but I soon figured it out when I walked into our room, and she and her mother were there, mouths open, looking at me like a deer in headlights.

Meanwhile, things didn't work out between Gene and me, but I was growing closer in friendship with Andy.

My new roommate and I wanted to decorate our room and needed transportation. Andy had a friend with a car, so he showed up one day with the keys to take us shopping in the Squirrel Hill section of Pittsburgh.

Marilyn needed to stop at the bank first. I remember there was a long line, and Andy, acting as our chauffeur for the day, sat in a chair while we waited. He suggested I sit on his lap since I didn't need to stand in line. To this day, Andy believes he was just being friendly with me, but throughout the day, I found him holding my hand and all of the little clues that hinted otherwise.

In time, the two of us were almost inseparable. We just hung out all the time. I also scheduled my classes around soap operas that I liked to watch. Well, I was a fan of *All My Children* and *Ryan's Hope*, and Andy wasn't a soap opera guy, but he'd spend that hour and a half with me in the dorm TV lounge during lunch watching those shows because he wanted to spend time with me. Andy eventually became addicted to soap operas, so that's kind of how we started our romance.

Andy took me on our first date to see the movie Flashdance, and afterwards, we had a romantic dinner at the top of the Incline at a restaurant called LeMont. He told me his family migrated here from Jamaica, West Indies, in 1976 when he was thirteen. That blew my mind because Andy didn't have a Jamaican accent. His parents decided to relocate their family in search of better opportunities. At the time, there was civil unrest there. They ended up in York, Pennsylvania, because his aunt and mother's sister lived in York, and there was a support system there. Andy has a younger brother who is two and a half years his junior.

Andy started school at St. Patrick's of York in the 7th grade. To blend in with the other students, he practiced "Americanizing" his accent so others could not deem him as different, so I did not detect it when I met him. He subsequently completed his high school education by attending York Catholic. He was a student-athlete who played both football and basketball. He also was an enthusiast of soccer, or football as they call it, in Jamaica. Andy excelled in sports and academics, which gave him several choices in deciding where to attend college and further his education. He graduated from York Catholic in May of 1982 and decided to participate in CMU to play football.

Talk about fate. What were the chances of two people from faraway areas choosing to attend the same college? Only God knew why.

Marilyn and I lived in a coed dorm called Morewood Gardens on the corner of campus, where you could walk right across the street for class. It was a lovely big old building that looked like it was once an old mansion that they converted into dorms. We also had neighbors, two guys who lived across from us. One of them, Lothair, was African American and a fine arts major. Lothair had the most prominent voice and was so dramatic. You could hear him in his room singing. He had a flair for drama and loved his mama, as he was a mama's boy. You know that saying, "Save the drama for your mama?" He kept me thoroughly entertained.

Another group of girls lived across the way, and Marilyn, who was never really comfortable with me, ended up being friends with one of those girls. The two female roommates across the hall had a scuffle, resulting in one of them moving out. One day, I returned from classes to discover Marilyn had just moved across the hall without telling me anything into the other girl's room. I remember feeling some kind of way, but I now had the room all to myself, so I didn't make a big stink about it. Andy and I were dating by then, so having the whole room was fine with me.

However, the same thing eventually happened to a girl I befriended. Her name was Patricia, but we called her Trish. She ended up having an altercation with her roommate, so I suggested that since we were friends and I had a vacancy in my room, she could come live with me.

I learned rather quickly that just because you're friends does not mean it will be like having this big slumber party. One of the lanes we had to learn how to navigate was that Trish would oversleep for her 8 AM classes all the time, saying, "G, can you please wake me up to make sure I don't miss my class."

Then what would happen? Whenever I tried to wake her, she would get mad at me, so I would say, "Fine. Go back to sleep!"

Carnegie Mellon did bring me more than my future husband. I found lifelong friends, including Don, Monet, Missy, Nita, Carl, Darral, and Ray. Don would later marry my dear friend Barbara. I'll tell you more about her later. Blair Underwood, the Blair Underwood, also attended CMU during my time there, and Andy and I enjoyed hanging out with him from time to time.

I was a varsity cheerleader my sophomore and part of my junior year. I also changed majors a few times but found that my highest grades were in math and computer science. This prompted me to major in Information and Decision Systems, a fancy way of saying Computer Science back then.

I struggled through a highly competitive program at CMU while participating in the work-study program to provide me with pocket change. Every time I visited my former school, Duchesne, during a school break, old teachers would ask me if I was back home, basically to stay. It helped give me the boost I needed to push through. Those teachers soon fueled my stubborn determination to succeed, and their silent desire to say, "I told you so," would not get the best of me. I had to fight through and deny them that pleasure.

Andy graduated from CMU in May of 1986 and moved to New Jersey to begin his first job with the Traveler's Insurance Company. I feared he would go into the real world and meet a real woman, leaving me in his rearview mirror.

I was in my senior year, determined to graduate on schedule. I needed to get to Andy. During that senior year, we talked endlessly on the phone. This was before cell phones, which meant whenever Andy called, I had to be in my room to talk to him or use a pay phone. It was more challenging to have a long-distance relationship back in 1986.

There was a place on campus called "The Cut," which was just greenery and open space. People would play Frisbee there all the time or sit on blankets to study and read and do whatever. Whenever I would return from class, I could see Andy's fraternity house in the distance. He lived there before graduating.

Andy would surprise me occasionally, not telling me he was coming to see me on certain weekends. I would be coming back from class all by myself, just walking through The Cut, and when I'd look up, I'd see Andy standing on the porch waiting for me. Moments like this reassured me that he was still engaged and interested.

As fate would have it, the day before I graduated with my B.S. in Information and Decision Systems in May 1987, Andy attended my graduation carrying a box of beautiful long-stemmed roses to congratulate me. My family had all gone on a tourist visit to Station Square to shop and eat, leaving my Aunt Margie, myself, and Andy in the hotel room. Aunt Margie couldn't wait to see the roses and insisted I open the box. When I did, while Aunt Margie saw 24 beautiful flowers of love, I could only see the beautiful engagement ring strategically tied and perched onto the bow that held them together. I could not believe it! I was getting engaged and would be Andy's wife! Of course, I said, "YES!"

With my family and a new fiancé there to support me during graduation, I could've dwelled on those who doubted that this day would come. But instead, I shifted my focus to my move to New Jersey with my future husband. I also had to begin wedding planning with my mom, which was a task since we were now living in New Jersey, but I wanted to get married in Texas. However, if you've come to learn anything about me, it's that I am driven to succeed.

So on the 28th day of May in 1988 in Houston, Texas, amongst three hundred guests, friends, and family, Andy and I were married and the next chapter of my life had begun.

TO GIA & ANDREW
TWO HEARTS – THEN ONE

On that beautiful summer afternoon at Carnegie Mellon,
we met.
We became colleagues, fond friends.
Faced challenges, persevered and came to love.
Love blossomed like a flower,
It sustained and brought us to this, Our finest hour....
Together, we share, love and grow.
We'll nourish our soul as beauty nourishes the simple rose.
With God's help, we will joyously express graciousness,
Kindness and love.
On this our wedding day
We are glad to have you share
And show us that you truly care.
As we go through the years
Our thoughts will give us pleasure.
And bring us back to us again.
To memories we shall gratefully treasure.

May 28, 1988
-Myrtle Ball Garrison, Mother of the Bride

CHAPTER 5
MY FIRST SPARK OF INTEREST

In 1991, Andy and I purchased our first home in Maplewood, New Jersey. I remember visiting it after looking at many homes in the area before falling in love with this cozy domicile. It was an older Cape Cod-style home on a quiet, tree-lined street with three bedrooms, two bathrooms, and a partially finished basement. This very suitable starter home was ideal for a young family on a budget, especially one leaving the apartment life where we resided during the first three years of our marriage. Once we closed on the house and settled in, we added a dog, a Sheltie named Caesar, and decided to start our family. Soon, I became pregnant with our first child. This time in our lives was exciting.

Since college, Andy and I had watched the soap operas for many years. I was drawn to a character on *Ryan's Hope* named Siobhan, pronounced Shiv-on, with a silent B. I also discovered that Siobhan is a feminine name of Irish origin, meaning God is gracious. Andy and I had decided that if we were to have a girl, we would name her Siobhan since we both took to the name. If we had a boy, we would call him Jourdan, a name I also loved.

Upon meeting all our new neighbors, I encountered a young couple named Yvonne and Eric, who lived diagonally across the street from us. They were also a young family, recently having their first child.

I remember the day Yvonne introduced me to her daughter, and guess what she said her name was? Shavon! *DAMN, DAMN, DAMN!* The only difference between their version and ours was how it was spelled. All I knew was that we couldn't go through with our plan and name our daughter Siobhan. Having two little girls on the same street with the same name felt inappropriate. So, I rethought my action plan, and we searched for a different girl's name.

My mother gave my brother and me names bearing the same initials, GLG. I liked this theme, and since my married name was now James, we decided on Jourdan Andrew James for our boy after Andy. I followed suit with this theme for a girl, and we agreed on Jazmyne Alexis James. I loved Jasmine Guy, who starred as Whitley in the hit television show *A Different World*. Yes, another television show character! We planned to spell the name differently than the traditional version to give the name a dash of personality.

As we awaited the birth of our first child, I discovered the joy of what it was like to have a baby growing inside of me. The immense love that I developed for my child before she was even born led me to question how any mother could carry a child for nine months and then give them away for adoption and never think of them again.

These emotions sparked questions in my mind that I never really considered before. Even when I'd notice a stranger point in my direction and say, "Doesn't she look so much like *so and so*?"

While growing up, people would either stop me or share this sentiment with others. It happened often, prompting me to start thinking about my heritage. *Who did I look like?* Are they talking about my sister? My mother? Someone who could be related to me?

That would also pique my interest, but I never had a genuine urge to dig deeper to explore my background. The primary reason I wanted to now search for my biological mother was to let her know that I was living a great life and all was wonderful. I wanted to reassure the woman who decided to give me away that her decision was a good one, although I never knew the circumstances under which I was placed for adoption. Except now, I wanted some of those questions to be answered.

It didn't help that while I was pregnant, I developed things like pregnancy-induced hypertension. We delivered a healthy baby girl named Jazmyne Alexis on October 1, 1992.

We moved to Rochester, New York, in 1994 because of Andy's job and discovered we were pregnant again. In 1995, Andy and I became the proud parents of another daughter whom we named Jordyne Ashleigh. This choice was initially tricky as we didn't know what to call another girl, but we still had the boy's name in mind. A friend suggested that we use our original boy name, Jordyne/Jourdan, notwithstanding the baby's gender since it was a unisex name.

During my pregnancy with Jordyne, I developed similar issues as I did with Jazmyne. We also found out during routine bloodwork that my physician performed that I was a carrier of beta-thalassemia.

Beta thalassemia is a condition that affects the production of hemoglobin in red blood cells, which is essential for transporting oxygen throughout the body. Individuals with this condition have lower oxygen levels due to reduced hemoglobin. It is vital for parents carrying the beta thalassemia trait to seek genetic counseling, as their children are at risk of inheriting the disease, which can cause significant fatigue.

And thank God Andy was not a carrier because now our only concern was that our children would be carriers like me.

When the nurse called me to tell me that I tested positive for the trait, she paused to ask, "Wait, aren't you Black?"

I replied, "Why yes."

"That's weird that you have this because it is more prevalent in people of Mediterranean or European descent," she informed me.

This posed more questions about my heritage and my genetic medical background. A few years later, I was diagnosed with hypertension at the age of about thirty-five, leading to those questions now haunting me. Was this something that I carried genetically?

I knew I needed to know for my family as much as myself, but I had no health history or record of it. I quickly realized that every time I went to the doctor and filled out all that medical history paperwork, whether for myself or my girls, I did not know any family history; therefore, I could never entirely give the doctors a clear picture of what they were dealing with when treating me.

Andy's job relocated us again, this time to the Chicago area. We moved our family into a rental property in

Wheaton, Illinois, in 1996 to get our bearings on the lay of the land before purchasing our second home.

Once I found new doctors to continue my care, I started taking medicine to regulate my hypertension at age thirty-five.

Soon, another test lurked around the corner. All I could do was place a question mark on the health history paperwork or leave it blank, just as it existed in my mind. Typically, women start having their baseline mammograms done at forty. My situation was very different, as we didn't know any of my background, so my doctors urged me to have my baseline mammogram and any other screenings done at age thirty-five instead.

Because of these new questions regarding my health, I finally spoke with my mother to find out what she knew about my adoption or if she had information regarding my birth parents. She said she had not been given anything as it was a closed adoption, but she did tell me the name of the agency that handled the adoption.

She then inquired why I was asking all these questions, and I could hear the concern in her voice. All my life, I knew her as my mother and never mentioned a need to seek anyone else, but I knew I had to have my "come to Jesus" talk with her about my desire to find my biological parents.

My mother appeared to be hurt at my need to find these things out, as if to question if she was not enough after selflessly raising me. I explained to her that my longing to find these answers was in no way to replace her, nor was it any expression that I was not grateful to her for everything she did for me. I just shared that she knew where *she* came from, *her* health history, who *she* resembled, *her* siblings, and everything surrounding *her* existence. I was missing all of this, and I likened it to putting together a 2000-piece jigsaw puzzle that is almost finished, only to find that there is a missing piece. I also told her I wanted her to be involved during every step of my search so there were no secrets. After discussing my stance ad nauseam, I convinced her to become my ally and vowed to share everything with her.

The following day, I contacted the Children's Bureau of New Orleans, the agency that handled my adoption. Although they still operate as the Children's Bureau of New Orleans, today, they no longer handle adoptions. I asked them if they could give me any information about my biological family. Their reply was an instant no, but they could give me what they called "non-identifying information" regarding my parents. This meant they could try to provide me with descriptions of what they looked like, possibly their ages, but no names would be given since the adoption records were closed. So I accepted this breadcrumb and waited for any information they could provide to arrive in the mail.

"The journey of a thousand miles begins with a single step." -Lao Tzu, Chinese Philosopher

---

Our first New Jersey home

CHAPTER 6
WHAT'S IN A NAME? WELL, I'LL TELL YOU...

It finally arrived!

The Children's Bureau of New Orleans sent me something, and I prayed it had the details about my biological parents. I anxiously opened it, and everything they could provide was given to me.

I discovered that my mother had me at the age of sixteen. Even more puzzling was that my father was thirty-nine! They listed his occupation as a painter, and his mother had a fair complexion with curly hair. From that information, I could decipher that how I was conceived was most likely non-traditional, and I wanted to learn more. Therefore, I quickly decided that I only wanted to find my mother so she could fill me in on how she became pregnant with me before deciding if I wanted to find my father. I also knew that when I was seeking this information, my father was most likely deceased, given the difference in their ages.

My biological grandfather was also thirty-nine then, so it was equally interesting that my birth father and grandfather were the same age!

As promised, I called my Mom and shared all the information I had received.

I later had an idea to get back in touch with the agency to see if I could persuade another door to open to help me get closer to discovering the truth. The person who answered the phone, who could have been the same person who helped me the first time, asked if I had a medical reason to get the records opened. They informed me that the ailments I mentioned weren't life-threatening or would prompt a judge to permit them to hand everything over.

Before you ask, I could've twisted the truth a little, but then I would have needed a lawyer to prove whatever I claimed to get the documents open. Unfortunately, since this did not apply to my situation, the only thing the lady I was speaking to could offer me secretly was the name and number of a person who used to be an employee at the Bureau of Vital Statistics in New Orleans. The agency employee asked me not to divulge that she had given me this information. I quickly hung up the phone with the Children's Bureau and immediately called her contact.

The woman I was referred to was also an adoptee, which is part of why she helped people like me and knew how to unlock the records. I found out that she was able to trace her records to identify her biological mother. We'll let her remain nameless but will call her "Tina."

When I spoke to Tina, she quickly explained how she worked. Tina would look up the information for me, which was illegal, but she said she could deliver it to me for a fee of $300, only payable by money order. Once Tina received my payment in the mail, she would call me with the information and share it verbally. I did as she requested, sent the money order, and waited.

About a week later, coming home after work, I got a phone call.

The caller asked, "May I speak to Siobhan?"

I replied, "You have the wrong number. There is nobody here by that name."

The caller then quickly replied, "Gia?"

"Yes, this is Gia."

It was Tina. "Gia, I discovered your name was Shevonne Marie, and your birth mother was Patricia Ann."

All the blood drained from my head, and I was speechless!

Remember how much I loved the name Siobhan and wanted to give that name to my firstborn? Was I attracted to the name Siobhan for all those years because it went deeper than just simply liking a name I heard on television? Deep down, I knew I was always drawn to it because it was *my given name, except* it was spelled S-H-E-V-O-N-N-E!

All I could think was that God put obstacles in my path to prevent me from naming Jazmyne Siobhan because it was *my* name! Fate was at work.

Tina told me that she had also found out some of the answers I was looking for and would assist me in contacting my birth mother by acting as a liaison. She explained to me that based on her own experience, after looking for her birth mother, once they finally met, she discovered that her mother was not well off. The woman was intimidated by her daughter showing up very well put together to an address in an area that let her know that her mother had been struggling. Because of this, Tina wanted to prepare me for all the possibilities of rejection I could face if we successfully attempted to contact her.

We then contacted several Patricia Anns in New Orleans, Louisiana, using "three-way calls." Whenever we encountered a person who answered, my heart would skip a beat while I remained silent, allowing Tina to speak on my behalf since she had experience in this type of mediation. We called about five different people and were still waiting for confirmation before retiring for the day.

A few days later, Tina called me back to say, after some additional research, she believed that my mother's name was Patricia Ann Brooks, and she found someone going by that name.

Patricia resided in a housing project in New Orleans where the only phone number was to a public telephone in the hallway. Remember, this was 1997. Cell phones were not widely available. The internet was a dial-up system called American Online. The information highway was a horse and buggy show. Tina's assistance was a godsend, and using technology was not an option.

Now, the two of us had to rely on whoever answered that hallway telephone to locate Patricia Ann Brooks and bring her to the phone.

Unfortunately, when someone did answer, the call did not materialize as we were on hold for quite a while just for the person to return and say they did not know her. Not giving in to disappointment, I put pen to paper and wrote to her instead. Hopefully, this would be the way I could successfully reach her.

My letter was complete with lots of thank you's for having me and facts about the happy life I had been living with my adopted family. I also enclosed pictures of Andy, myself, and our children so Patricia could see we were okay and provided an image of what we all looked like.

Tina allowed me to use her post office box as the return address. This way, my address would be protected if my advances were unwelcome. But before mailing the letter, I read it to my mother, who was still on this journey with me, who thought the letter was well-written and thought out.

Tina and I waited for weeks without a reply. Then weeks turned into months, and by this time, I had lost all hope of a reunion with my birth mother. The ball was no longer in my court, and I had no other plays.

"Failure is only the opportunity to begin again, this time more intelligently." - Henry Ford

---

CHAPTER 7
MY CURIOSITY PIQUED

As the next year passed, internet development improved, and now I longed to find my family. I wondered what had happened to my adoptive father, Isaac Peter Garrison, III. The last thing I remembered was that he was living in Louisiana.

One day, while searching the internet for him, I got a hit. It turns out that he was now living in Chicago. This was the last place I expected to find him – in my backyard. As I dialed the number listed, my mind was racing, my hands were trembling, and my mouth was dry. If he answered, what was I going to say?

A gentleman answered, "Hello."

"May I please speak with Pete?" I asked.

There was a bit of a pause before he replied, "He is not here right now. Can I ask who this is?"

Something in me recognized his voice. This was my father, but why was he acting shifty? Was he in trouble or hiding from something or someone?

Uncertain, I was not ready to reveal myself to the person on the other end. "I must have the wrong number."

Then, I quickly hung up.

Time passed, but the conversation stayed on my mind. On Easter Sunday, I decided to call the number again. After the same familiar voice answered, I tried again, "May I please speak with Pete."

"Who is this?" the voice asked.

I didn't answer, choosing to ask to speak to Pete again. His reluctance to reveal himself to me persisted, so I laid it on him.

"Daddy, this is Gia, your daughter."

The man paused, an audible gasp letting me know he was stunned, and I could only imagine whoever was on the other end probably looked as if I had slapped them in the face.

"Really?!" my father asked, so I confirmed that it was me.

Daddy had lots of questions, and I supplied the answers. I told him that I was now married and had two daughters, his granddaughters, and we were living west of Chicago. He greedily wanted to see me, and I could tell he hoped to start this instant Daddy/Daughter relationship.

Somehow, I gathered my thoughts and explained to him that it was too late for that type of relationship as I no longer needed a father. I merely reached out to him to satisfy my curiosity and to inquire why he decided not to participate in me and my brother's lives.

As we spoke, I asked him a series of prying questions based on the nature of our severed relationship.

Why didn't you keep in touch? Why didn't you pay child support as the court ordered you to? Are you still drinking?

Each question was either explained away or avoided, or I received an answer I knew had to have been a lie.

I wanted to tell him that watching my mother struggle

to raise us always reminded me of his absence. That fueled my desire to have a family of my own. Understanding the importance of each parental role in the familial unit and my recent need to find my biological mother all contributed to why I reached out to him.

I then asked him, "Are you gay?"

When we were younger, my brother told me that our father was gay. I never witnessed anything that eluded to that being true; nevertheless, I let it fly out of my mouth as if that could explain something unknown I was seeking. He denied it, so I also let that question go.

Daddy said he wanted to see me and invited my family and me to schedule a day to visit Chicago. He wanted to treat us to brunch or dinner. Despite telling him I didn't want to reestablish our father/daughter relationship, I granted his request. After coordinating and planning, we drove to the south side of Chicago on a sunny Sunday afternoon after church to see him. Andy, the girls, and I picked up my father in front of his home and went to a nearby park, which felt like good neutral territory for this small family reunion. That's where we sat on a park bench and visited so I could introduce him to my family. We also took a photo to memorialize the occasion. Jazmyne and Jordyne were very young and most likely did not remember that day; however, I told them that he was their grandfather so they could have the chance to know him in their lives.

After a while, we migrated to a nearby restaurant he recommended for an early dinner and ate. Toward the end of the meal and through our conversation, I deduced that he was very down on his luck and still was experiencing some financial difficulty by the way he presented himself.

We ended up paying for the meal and driving him home. Daddy invited us into his apartment in the rear of a building. The only means of entry to his place was walking through an alley and climbing the stairs from the outside.

The apartment seemed well lived in, and his roommate, Johnny, appeared and introduced himself. It was apparent to me that Johnny was very effeminate, which confirmed to me that what my brother told me was most likely accurate, as other reports indicated Johnny was probably more than a roommate. However, my Dad wouldn't openly acknowledge him as anyone significant to him. I'm confident this is why his marriage to my mother did not work out. Once we finished our visit, I decided that I would never go to see him again. In my opinion, he was still not living an honest life and wanted to continue to pull the wool over my eyes, and I refused to continue to make myself available to be lied to after all this time.

Andy and I purchased our second home on Westhaven Circle in Geneva, Illinois, and moved our family from the rental on Champion Forest Court in 1997. We loved the new cul-de-sac and neighborhood. I started working as a software developer for Accenture in Saint Charles, Illinois, and the kids were attending a local elementary school.

As the years progressed, my father's health declined. We did speak periodically over the phone, but I never visited. When he was hospitalized, Johnny was at his side, calling me diligently to inform me of Dad's health. My father's alcoholism finally took its toll after all the years he abused his body.

Johnny begged me to visit the hospital since things did not look good for him, and my father was asking for me. I just told Johnny I could not bring myself to be there for my father after all the years he was not there for me, but to please keep me informed of any news. My father passed away two days before Christmas on December 23, 1999. The cause of death listed on his death certificate was upper gastrointestinal bleeding and bacterial sepsis.

Since Dad had no next of kin, I was it. I needed to make sure that he was buried. His friends and some of his family in the area assisted me in making the funeral plans, but they needed additional funds to carry them out. My father accumulated little to no real money, but Johnny told me he had a few accounts. I took my birth certificate as proof that I was his daughter, the death certificate, and my marriage license to those financial institutions to gather up his money and give it to the family along with a little extra out of my pocket to get the job done.

I took a day off to attend his funeral at the funeral home. Johnny greeted me at the door, and they ushered me up to the reserved seating at the front during the viewing. Before taking my designated place, I looked down at my father in the coffin and was sort of void of emotion. Yes, that was my father, the man who adopted me. I was thankful to him for rescuing me and assisting in carrying out my biological mother's wish of helping me escape the hands of my birth father and placing me in the arms of my nurture mother, Myrtle.

Hearing various people come up during the funeral and say glowing things about my father was foreign to me since I had not heard positive things about him all my life. If allowed to approach the podium to say a few words, I would respectfully decline as I had nothing positive to say.

Since Pete was a veteran who served in the Air Force, he was interred at the Abraham Lincoln National Cemetery in Joliet, Illinois, on January 4, 2000. The flag draped over his coffin was ceremoniously folded and presented to me. In addition to his death certificate, I still possess the flag. Besides the fact that my father married my mother and agreed to adopt me, in addition to the picture we captured that day on the park bench, it is the only thing I possess to date that represents him.

CHAPTER 8
VIVID MEMORIES

In early 2001, our dog Caesar turned eight years old, so Andy and I welcomed Roman, another Sheltie, to our family.

When Roman was about five months old, he escaped from the leash during a walk in the neighborhood and ran away from home into a nearby cornfield. We formed a search party to look for him before nightfall but were unsuccessful. Coyotes were known to roam around at night, and small dogs sometimes were reported missing. The girls and I were so concerned that we would not be able to get Roman home safely and were sick with worry.

As the next day dawned, I resumed my search for Roman, unable to concentrate at work. I needed to take advantage of the daylight before it got dark. His breeder and I spoke, and she suggested I also inform the police and the veterinarian in case someone brought him into the office. He was microchipped, so we hoped that if he were found, he would be returned to us as soon as possible. The search party members grew with each hour, and by day two, we had about twenty people searching for him and calling his name.

There were sightings of him, but as we closed in, he got spooked and fled. How were we going to get him back? He was impossibly fast, and the cornfield was enormous, spanning almost 350 acres.

We split up into even smaller parties and took our cell phones so we could communicate with each other. We needed to get Roman before the coyotes had him for dinner. As the day passed, I grew increasingly concerned that we would not get Roman back, and hope started to fade. We were in love with our new puppy, and I could not bear to explain his absence to the girls. By now, Jazmyne and Jordyne were 8 and 5 years old and would have this terrible memory.

During day three of the search, I was out in the cornfield and received an incoming call. As I answered, all I could hear was cheering in the background. On the other end was a group of neighbors saying they had captured Roman in our *yard!* The poor thing got so hungry and tired that he had reached his breaking point, risked crossing over the busy street, sat down in the backyard, and waited. Some of the neighborhood kids were out playing and happened to spot him. They quickly and quietly cornered him. Roman was too tired to move and gave in. He was done running.

You have to understand that living in Geneva, Illinois, was a carefree life, and not many things happened that far west of Chicago. It was a smaller, close-knit, bedroom community, tranquil and almost devoid of hard crimes. The small things mattered, and people cared for one another, so people were interested in helping us find Roman and bring him back safely.

We celebrated Roman's safe return home, and the story

gained popularity. Soon, a local Kane County Chronicle reporter called me for an interview. I gladly accepted the invitation and even suggested the title for the article when she came to the house to meet the family and the dogs.

A few mornings later, my good friend and next-door neighbor, Crystal, called me at the crack of dawn, telling me to look at that day's edition of the paper. I went out to retrieve it, and there we were on the headline page, above the fold of the May 11, 2001 edition of the Kane County Chronicle, with a huge picture and *my* suggested title, "Roamin' Roman."

61

In July 2001, our days of living in Geneva ended as my husband secured another excellent employment opportunity with Pfizer in New York City. We would come full circle, relocate back to our beloved Maplewood, New Jersey, and purchase a home on Wyoming Avenue, a much larger house than the one we started in on Porter Road. We could stand on the second floor and see the Empire State Building in the distance. We were "moving on up" like George and Louise Jefferson. We closed on August 24, 2001, and Andy started commuting daily via the Midtown Direct into New York City as his office was on 42nd Street in their Corporate Headquarters. Little did we know that our whole world would change in a few weeks.

On the morning of September 11, 2001, I was still unpacking, and the California Closet guys were installing custom closets in the house so I could finally get the girl's clothes unpacked and settled in. They were both at school. Andy called to inform me that a plane had flown into one of the towers of the World Trade Center.

I immediately ran to the television and witnessed with horror as the events of the day unfolded. We lost the ability to call and communicate with people via cell phone, so I was worried that something would happen to my husband. One of his cousins, Beverly, worked in one of those towers, and I briefly spoke with her ex-husband, Vernel, to get an update on whether she made it out safely. The uncertainty of how many people would not return home was genuine.

I started asking myself, "Lord, why did you move me and my family back to this God-forsaken East Coast area with all this going on!" The school called and told the parents if we wanted to come and pick up our children, we could do so; however, I waited until school was over to retrieve them because I did not want them to view the broadcasts and worry about their father.

Vernel let me know he had gotten in touch with Beverly; she was safe and alive after barely making it out of the towers. It was such a relief.

Soon, New York Transit blocked all subway access in and out of the city, and I did not know if Andy had made it out safely. Later that evening, there was a gentle knock at the back door. My good friend and old Porter Road next-door neighbor, Marie, also worked in New York. Marie was shaken as she inquired if I heard from Andy and if he was ok. I told her that Andy had just gotten through to me and was fine but now stuck in the city. Andy stayed with an old and dear college friend, Laura, that night. Laura had been on the street and witnessed firsthand when the second plane collided with the final tower. I was glad that Andy was there to stay at her New York apartment as everyone was coping with the total shock.

After retrieving the kids from school, I informed them that their father was fine but not able to leave the city due to the shutdown.

The following morning, after dropping the girls off at school, Andy came through our back door, and I was so relieved to see him safely home that I ran and threw my arms around him. We discussed what had just occurred the day before, and I went upstairs to resume unpacking boxes as I needed something to quiet my mind after all that was happening.

We knew that all the flights had been grounded, and there was silence in the skies above. Suddenly, I heard a loud rumbling, and the house shook. I fell to my knees out of fear because I did not know if another terrorist attack was occurring. The sound was so loud as it approached and went directly over the house. I just waited for the impact of whatever it was and cried out to Andy. He ran upstairs and told me that I heard military fighter jets flying over our home from the city.

The next few weeks were filled with sad stories of families who lost someone during the tragedy. A sense of heaviness and deep sorrow hung over the East Coast area that can't be described. To live in this part of the country during that time seemed unreal.

To top things off, I fell outside my home on September 25th and splintered my right ankle, requiring surgery to repair it. All I could think about during the entire ordeal was how would I get my family settled into our new home now? I could'nt drive and needed to get my daughters to and from school because no school buses were available. Why was this all happening to me?

Fortunately, my mother flew in to assist me during my surgery and recovery. Everything was going well with her. Then, one Saturday, I was unpacking some boxes in my dining room. People started showing up. Friends and family appeared and dropped by out of the blue at various times throughout the day. It was like a revolving door. I could now see God showed me why He directed our steps back to Maplewood.

This was where most of our friends and family were, and we had so much love and support. It all made sense. God knew this was where we needed to be at *this* particular time in our lives when it seemed like the world was going mad, and He knew to break my ankle to make me appreciate it.

I obtained my real estate license during the six years in

our Wyoming Avenue home. I became a very successful real estate agent with Burgdorff Realtors, the agency we used to purchase both our Porter Road and Wyoming Avenue homes. It was a rewarding career for me, and I enjoyed the people I met and the new friends we made.

We loved entertaining with all our friends, new and old. In time, receiving a coveted invitation to our annual Crawfish Boil was well sought after, and we enjoyed having everyone over for a delectable Creole-seasoned seafood boiled with andouille sausage, potatoes, and corn. The connection to my Louisiana roots was still very evident in my life.

My Superbowl Gumbo was also a special request of Andy's and always our tradition on the big game day. We were happy, and life was rewarding in many ways.

"Angels live among us. Sometimes, they hide their wings, but there is no disguising the peace and hope they bring."
- Unknown

CHAPTER 9

DOOMSDAY, OR SO I THOUGHT...

In 2003, during my recovery from an elective surgical procedure, Andy had to travel to Sweden on business. His mother assisted me with the kids while he was abroad. Renovations of bathrooms were underway, and we had temporarily moved to the finished basement to sleep in a dust-free zone.

One late night, I started having difficulty inhaling, which was very odd since I had never had asthma or any breathing-related illnesses before. I went to my home library for the *Complete Guide to Symptoms, Illness & Surgery* by H. Winter Griffith, M.D., which helped me diagnose things for my children while they were growing up. This guide did the trick in helping me understand what symptoms were serious and what the suggested remedy might be.

I referenced my symptom, breathing difficulty, at the front of the book on page thirty-nine. One of the factors read, "Sudden breathing difficulty. Sharp pain in the chest that worsens with inhalation."

Under possible problems related to this symptom, it read, "Blood clot in the lung. Collapsed lung."

Under what to do, it said, "Call a doctor now. See Pulmonary Embolism."

Of course, I did as the doctor suggested and flipped to the Pulmonary Embolism page for further explanation. It said the risk increases with "recent surgery," amongst other items. *BINGO!*

The instructions said I should call my doctor immediately if I had these symptoms. *"This is an emergency!"*

It was the middle of the night, but I wanted to call my mother to seek her advice. When I uttered the words pulmonary embolism, she urged me to hang up the phone and get to the hospital at once. Because of the recent surgery, I could not operate a vehicle, so I called my friend, Barbara, who picked me up immediately. Within ten minutes, we were en route to Overlook Hospital, which is where I had my recent surgery performed. They would have my patient records readily available, and hopefully, this could aid in my treatment.

When we walked in at approximately two in the morning, the emergency room was virtually empty. I was immediately assisted and explained my situation and what I had just read in the medical reference guide, making sure to let them know that I wanted to rule out a pulmonary embolism.

The necessary steps were performed, and by about six o'clock, the staff came in and asked me about the reference guide and how I reached my diagnosis. I reiterated my process and was sure they would tell me to go fly a kite and that everything was fine. To my surprise, they said, "We are so glad you did that because, yes, you sure have one."

Barbara and I were in total shock. I gasped and started tearing up. If I had ignored my symptoms, like so many people do, and stayed at home, I could have dropped *dead* at any moment!

Suddenly, there was chaos as the medical team rushed in to admit me and save my life. IVs were being connected, injections were shooting into me, and I had to sign paperwork. As things were being prepared for my readmission to the hospital, the surgeon who had performed the recent procedure burst into the room and exclaimed, "Gia, are you trying to scare me?!"

He removed my drainage tubes so they would not interfere with my new diagnosis.

Barbara informed Andy of what was happening, and he was on the next flight smoking from Sweden. For the next five days, I was on an IV drip of blood thinners and oxygen as my levels were subpar. Besides childbirth, this was one of the most painful processes I ever went through. The pain endured from the blood clot dissolving, plus the difficulty breathing, which we take for granted and is involuntary, was something I would not wish on anyone. I thanked God for sparing my life, knowing He was not done with me yet. There was a reason He saved my life.

After this incident, I was able to use my experience to save another person from a pulmonary embolism. A friend who knew what I had experienced called me to inquire about my symptoms, and the doctors were able to save that patient as well.

Later that year, we lost our beloved first dog, Caesar. He was 14 years old. Deciding to put him down was sudden and brutal. We added a third Sheltie puppy to the family and named him Simba. Roman was the dutiful protector of Simba and showed him the ropes. Simba quickly picked up our house etiquette and was easily potty trained. He was an excellent addition to the James Gang.

Life continued at lightning speed, and the kids grew and prospered. Jordyne was in the sixth grade and Jazmyne was now in the eighth grade. The end of their school year was around the corner when, in 2007, Andy was offered a new job with Wyeth Pharmaceuticals in Collegeville, Pennsylvania, a small town outside of Philadelphia. We waited for the girls to finish school so we could smoothly transition them from one school to another. Since Jazmyne was entering high school, she would attend a new school anyway.

I went to preview homes in the area with my mother and fell in love with the house we currently live in. We made our plans and relocated again. In school, Jazmyne played basketball, and Jordyne was on the soccer team. They graduated in 2010 and 2012, respectively. Jazmyne attended Auburn University and graduated with a B.S. in Animal Sciences. Jordyne attended the University of Maryland and received her B.S. in Psychology and B.A. in Family Science. They are both pursuing higher degrees at Colorado State and Pepperdine University. Andy and I are beaming with pride.

I am now retired by choice and very active with my sorority while caring for my mother-in-law. There is never a dull moment.

Our second New Jersey home

CHAPTER 10
OMAR

After many years of waiting for Patricia Ann Brooks' reply, I resolved that nothing would be forthcoming. My family moved three times: first to Geneva, Illinois, then to Maplewood, New Jersey, and finally to Collegeville, Pennsylvania. My husband's career was very lucrative, and we were grateful for all his opportunities. Jazmyne was now in high school, and Jordyne was entering the seventh grade, so life was progressing quickly. However, I never gave up hope that my search would resume to find my biological mother. The internet and level of technology had advanced enough over those years that I could quickly do Google searches to find out information on anything and almost everything.

One afternoon in late 2012, I decided to Google "Patricia Ann Brooks" to see what I could pull up. An obituary for "Patricia Brooks" appeared in the search results.

Reading it, I discovered that she passed away in 2008. She was also a mother to a son, leaving a host of nieces, nephews, and relatives.

And maybe even me.

I immediately felt sad, but I returned to the name listed for her son. Omar Brooks. Could he be my brother? I did an online search with no immediate results. I changed course and looked for him on Facebook. Initially, I did not find a match there, but this would lead me to do a similar search every six months or so.

I struck gold in 2013 and found Omar Alphonse Brooks on LinkedIn and Facebook, so I immediately sent him messages through both platforms. The message I sent through LinkedIn yielded no response, but I had some luck on Facebook.

On January 17, 2013, I sent Omar my first communication and told him my history and my theory of him being my half-brother. He responded on the same day, and his tone was somewhat that of a dazed and confused person, as expected. I reiterated my stance and waited for his next reply.

The next day, upon checking my messages and not receiving a reply from Omar, I made another attempt to ask him if he received my previous message.

Omar replied in the affirmative and said he would love to see if this was true because his mom passed away in 2008. Then he provided his telephone number and asked me to call.

Once I returned home, I called and spoke to Omar for the first time. I told him my story and that I had written to his mother in an attempt to contact her during my search, but it was many years ago, and I never received a reply from her. That's when he gave me some details about Patricia and the circumstances around her death.

She died suddenly from either a stroke or a heart attack at home, and Omar was there with her as she transitioned. Omar went on to tell me that he was her only child.

After Patricia's death, Omar had to clear out her things from her home and, in doing so, discovered that she had a box of keepsakes under her bed. As he went through the box's contents, he found the letter I had written her all those years ago! He further explained that after he discovered the letter, he asked several aunts and uncles about the validity of it. None would verify it, saying that they did not remember.

That's when I realized that I had written the correct woman and that Omar's confirmation of discovering the letter after Patricia's death was proof enough to both of us that we were indeed brother and sister. All the math was adding up. Omar was also two years younger than me, so it was all possible.

Omar and I continued our relationship throughout the years by talking periodically and texting each other. He would regularly post pictures of himself and Patricia on Facebook, and I would selfishly save them to my phone's photos just so I could have a piece of her in my life.

However, I was still unsure when people asked me if I looked like Patricia. To me, there was no real resemblance. All I knew was she was my mother, and without having a picture of my biological father and the fact that Patricia was now deceased, I would never have a real conclusion.

Omar referred to me as "Sis" during our talks, although we never met in person. However, the lines of communication remained open throughout the next ten years, and we were content with our relationship with no other questions asked.

That's why I never second-guessed whether Omar was my brother: All the pieces fit. He had discovered the letter that I had written Patricia all those years ago tucked away amongst her most personal possessions, so he had to be the correct person. Right?

CHAPTER II
IT'S IN THE DNA

A round this time, Ancestry.com started to take off as commercials and testimonies of how people could send in their DNA samples and get information about their heritage gained popularity. This intrigued me so much because there were still many answers that I longed for. Therefore, I purchased a kit and joined Ancestry on August 30, 2016.

Once my results were processed and uploaded to the site the day after my birthday, which was two months later, I found out what my DNA revealed in their report regarding my ethnicity:

Your DNA looks most like DNA from these 13 world regions. We compare your DNA against a worldwide reference panel to see which populations your DNA looks most like.

- *Cameroon, Congo & Western Bantu Peoples - 23%*
- *Nigeria - 17%*
- *Mali - 13%*
- *Benin & Togo - 13%*
- *Ireland - 12%*

- *Senegal - 7%*
- *Sweden & Denmark - 6%*
- *Ivory Coast & Ghana - 3%*
- *Germanic Europe - 2%*
- *Nigeria, East Central - 1%*
- *Northern Africa - 1%*
- *Indigenous Americas - North - 1%*
- *Scotland - 1%*

Hmmm, what did all of this mean? How should I interpret it? Basically, this was a list of mumbo jumbo that told me what I already generally knew! I always knew that I was a descendant of Africa and a Black woman! I watched Roots with LeVar Burton and Alex Haley, DUH! Why did I spend all that money on this kit?

Then I looked at my DNA matches on the Ancestry site to see if there were any new revelations, but I didn't recognize any at the time. This left me feeling somewhat baffled at what I was looking at and disappointed by what it all could mean, so I focused on printing out my heritage piece and continued on with my daily activities.

Years passed before Ancestry reentered my sphere and occupied my frontal lobe, even though I continued to receive solicitation emails from them. My guess is that over time, I became desensitized to them.

In 2022, I received an email message from Ancestry informing me that I had some unread messages. Until then, I considered most of their emails spam, but this time, it felt different. It had been so long that I didn't even know if I remembered my login credentials.

It took several attempts to log in, but I finally was successful. That's when I found a message that was sent to me back in October 2016—six years ago!

My name is Stephanie, and you and I share DNA. Our family is from Southeast Louisiana and the river parishes of Louisiana. We have strong roots in south Mississippi, and I have traced us back to Alabama, Georgia, South Carolina, and specifically, North Carolina, Virginia, and Maryland, especially Prince George County.

Have you considered uploading your raw data to gedmatch? Gedmatch is a free service and a unique tool that allows you to upload your data from your testing company and then compare your DNA with others in the system who have done the same. If you tested with Ancestry, you will see those who shared their data from Ancestry and those from 23andMe and family tree DNA. Additionally, gedmatch allows you to see the exact chromosome and segment of that chromosome where the match is. Finally, DNA is random, and I would like to see if you match other family members. They tested with 23andMe, and I have their data on gedmatch.

The Ancestry messaging system has its flaws, so you may also reach me at... (She supplied her email address.)

I hope to hear from you.

This message was sent to me five days after I viewed my original DNA results from a fifth to eighth cousin on my paternal family side. As you can imagine, I was pretty frustrated because I never saw her message, and so much time had passed.

On July 2, 2022, which was six years after she initially sent her message to me, I responded with the following email:

Hello Stephanie,
I have not been on Ancestry for some time. However, I just saw your message. Yes, I am adopted, but was born in New Orleans, Louisiana. I have never met any biological relatives and would love to find out more. This is my personal email, and I have put my phone number below...

Stephanie Quiette-Addison Martin called me, and we talked for a long time. We somehow realized we were connected through our DNA but did not know how. Nevertheless, she offered to assist me in my search for the truth.

Stephanie described her motivation as a hobby and that she, too, had an estranged family, half-siblings, and so forth. Her passion for reuniting relatives with one another was what she liked to accomplish. Therefore, I informed her about Omar and that he was my half-brother and gave her permission to enter my account so she could access my family tree. This would help her assist me further in getting closer to completing the research and connecting the dots.

I need to rewind a few years to give you a broader picture so you can understand even more of my reasoning. In 2018, I stumbled across a movie called "Our Father" that aired on Netflix. Our Father was based on a true story about a fertility doctor named Dr. Donald Cline who used his sperm on his patients during the 1970s and 1980s without their knowledge or consent. The documentary followed how one woman discovered she had dozens of half-siblings, and that was the catalyst pushing her down a rabbit hole that unraveled everything. Her discovery led to the number of siblings growing to - get this... 94 half-brothers and sisters! All this is because they bought kits and deposited their DNA into the database to get their matches. The information gathered is also what ultimately led to Dr. Cline's prosecution.

I became so engrossed in this story that I soon purchased my own 23andMe DNA kit to seek more answers.

Would their brand yield more matches?

My results arrived that June, and I quickly went to work viewing them. There were repeats of what I found in Ancestry, but this time, I had new DNA matches that were different than what was reported before. To my dismay, nothing earth-shattering or surprising appeared, as no high matches were available. I decided to log out once again and went on about my life.

I also gave Stephanie access to my 23andMe account, along with the other account, hoping she could make sense of it all.

Over the years, more DNA matches appeared. My highest match was an 84-year-old woman named Audrey Bean, who lived in Pittsburg, California. Our relationship was defined as a first cousin, once removed, and we shared 6.82% DNA.

Audrey also contacted me asking, "Who are your relatives in Baton Rouge, LA?"

I replied to tell her that I was adopted, but I believe my birth mother had the maiden name of Brooks. I shared that I was born in New Orleans and that I never knew who my birth father was. I did share that he was significantly older than my mother, with her being sixteen at the time. I also shared that my biological father was a thirty-nine-year-old painter, and his mother, my grandmother, had fair skin and blue eyes.

I let Audrey know she was my highest match on 23andMe, and as with everyone else I've connected with thus far, I hope to find answers.

A month later, Audrey replied:

I was born in Baton Rouge. My paternal grandmother (Mamie Franklin) was fair skin, but no blue eyes. My maternal grandparents were Bell and William Tilley. Do you know from which side we are first cousins? I don't think it's from the maternal side because my uncles all lived in Baton Rouge. Hope this helps, but if you find out more, be sure to let me know.

Me:

Hello, I believe it is from the paternal side. My biological father could have been your uncle or father. Not sure. The blue eyes may be inaccurate. Can you send me a picture of you so I can see what you look like? I have a picture on my profile. Do we have similar features? I am on Eastern time, so bear in mind I am 3 hours ahead of you.

I supplied my phone number and asked her to call if she would like to talk.

Cousin Audrey called me, and we spoke for about half

an hour, discussing relatives we could have had in common. She thought my father could be one of the Franklin men in her family, and she proceeded to name them all: Percy, John, Charlie (Audrey's Father), Snook, Daniel, Joseph, and Willie. She said that there were also two sisters, Ruby and Thelma and that everyone was now deceased.

Audrey and I decided to stay in touch, and she said she would gladly assist me if she could.

It was amazing that Stephanie and Audrey's willingness to reach out and connect to me, a total stranger, was directly tied to the fact that we shared DNA. The strong family ties that are intertwined connect the leaves and branches.

Over the next few months, I kept in touch with Stephanie and Audrey to keep the lines of communication open.

CHAPTER 12
WAIT... WHAT?!

One evening, I was sitting on the sofa watching television when I received a text message from Stephanie.

"Call me."

I immediately picked up the phone to do just that, and she revealed that during her research, she could not figure out how Omar was connected to my family tree.

After we discussed possible scenarios, Stephanie asked me, "Do you think that Omar would agree to take a DNA test?"

I told her he would since he believed he was my brother. We decided that would be the best protocol instead of asking him to get his uncle or his mother's close relatives to do it. If Omar and I were to match up as siblings, his DNA would unlock the key to confirm things.

Once I spoke with Omar and explained to him that since a few of his relatives now knew about the possibility of my existence and had contacted me, questions were now circling, and we needed to confirm our relationship. He was willing to take the Ancestry.com DNA test as predicted, so I had it mailed to him.

We were again in a holding pattern, waiting for his results to be processed. Omar informed me when the lab had received his sample, and the results were promised to arrive by December 5, 2022.

December 5th quickly came and went, so I contacted Omar to see if his results were in. I had yet to receive him as a new match on my Ancestry profile and wondered what was holding things up.

Omar finally confirmed that his results had been revealed and needed clarification about what to look for because he could not see that I was a match for him, nor did he recognize any of his current matches.

My next call was to Stephanie, who suggested that I should send Omar the 23andMe kit to see if that test manifested any matches with me. Stephanie said that if anything happened to Omar's test in transit, having the backup results using 23andMe would solidify whether there was a DNA match.

After informing Omar that he would receive the new kit in the mail, I ordered it for him. As promised, he took the test and sent it in. After those results came in at the beginning of January 2023, it was confirmed he was *not* a match.

Oh my Lord, Omar was NOT my brother! I could not believe what we thought for the last ten years was untrue! We were not siblings, after all, and my heart was broken. What was I supposed to do now? On top of no longer having the one person I thought connected me to my biological mother, I was now back to square one.

The overwhelming feeling of loss and defeat was more than I could stand. How could I explain to Omar that although he had accepted me as his big sis for the last ten years, it was a mistake? Telling him this news was hard because I did not want to hurt him or leave him feeling empty-handed.

Eventually I would need to have this conversation with Omar, but for now, I needed to focus on my next steps.

In the meantime, Stephanie was also trying to figure out where to direct me. During our conversation a few days later, she told me she had a good friend who happened to be a professional genealogist. That friend gave her some information to guide me in my next steps.

I discovered that in Louisiana, the Governor recently signed Act No. 470 of the 2022 Legislative Regular Session, providing adopted persons twenty-four years or older access to their original birth certificate.

Since 1977, adoptees could only obtain their birth certificates through court orders. The new act, which became law effective August 1, 2022, created a simplified process allowing an adopted person to request a non-certified copy of their birth certificate without going to court. The revision of the law also allows birth parent(s) to submit a Contact Preference Form indicating whether they would like to be contacted directly or through an intermediary or not at this time. The form would be placed in a sealed file, and when the original birth record is requested, it would be sent to the applicant.

Stephanie then emailed me the application to request a Pre-Adoption Birth Certificate from The State Registrar and Vital Statistics office. If I met specific criteria, this would help me secure my original birth certificate.

When I received her email on January 9, 2023, I went to the website listed to eagerly make the request. While following her instructions, I noticed that Stephanie's email signature included quotes that still stand out to me today.

> "An ancestor never dies till there is no one left to call their name."

> "Be kinder than necessary, for everyone you meet is fighting some kind of battle." ~Yoruba Proverb

I admit that although I was eager about the potential of this latest development, I still had to pull my strength together to continue and begin the process. I told myself that I couldn't just give up.

Could my biological mother still be alive? Could I have other brothers and sisters? She would only be in her seventies, according to the math, which was feasible. Once I filled out the application and gathered all the required documents, I prepared the envelope for the mail that night to send off the following day.

The reality that I would play the waiting game again left an uneasy feeling in the pit of my stomach. What if they received my application and rejected it by saying they could not honor my request? What if, what if?!!!!

CHAPTER 13

FINDING MY TRIBE... AGAIN!

S ince the day I was born, I've been fortunate to have found family in many ways. I gained family through my adoption, the tribe I bonded with at Carnegie Mellon, and the sisters I've connected with through my sorority, Alpha Kappa Alpha. One of my sorority sisters is Tammie, whom I met through Barbara.

Barbara and Tammie were neighbors. Barbara knew how much we had in common, from hobbies to family dynamics, and in 2005, she believed we should meet.

Our families became friends very quickly. We just melded together from day one. Then, we became even closer because Barbara moved to North Carolina, and I moved to Pennsylvania, which put me near Tammie. We ultimately decided to join an interest group to start a new chapter for Alpha Kappa Alpha, and therein lies where Tammie and I started spending a lot more time together and became close.

Despite our closeness, I don't know why I didn't tell either of my best friends or even my husband that I filed the paperwork to get a copy of my original birth certificate. I don't believe it was intentional. In hindsight, perhaps I was being protective of everyone's emotions. I'd gone through so much during this search, one I originally had no intentions of doing, but everyone was along for the ride with me. I just knew that I couldn't afford another emotional twist or turn that disappointed us all.

I was waiting forever to receive the response regarding my application, checking the mail daily like a it was a refund check. Funny thing about the mail, the United States Postal Service (USPS) offers a feature called informed delivey where, via email, you can receive a preview of what will be arriving to your mailbox that very day. These were actual photos of the letters, bills, and junk mail that were coming. Once I subscribed to this service, I was able to prepare myself emotionally for what was to arrive. And so, on March 1, 2023, instead of just feeling eager to get the news, I felt relieved yet guarded at the same time when I saw the letter in my preview email.

What would the letter say? Was Tina mistaken all those years ago with the information she gave me over the phone? Was my name even Shevonne Marie, as I had thought all these years? Who was I? Who was my mother? Was there a chance she was still living? My heart skipped a beat from all the nervousness.

I believed that area of the home was the ideal place to park myself because our kitchen faces a side street, where the mail truck's distinctive sound can be heard and viewed as it goes down the cul-de-sac to deliver the daily mail and packages.

As I waited, my husband, Andy, entered the kitchen, and I began to tell him I would receive my original birth certificate that day. Andy cheered "Yay" to my declaration, but it wasn't his Dallas Cowboys winning the Super Bowl. "Yay," it was the Philadelphia Eagles winning the Super Bowl." Andy could care less about the Philadelphia Eagles, and in this moment, he could care less about my original birth certificate or me.

Granted, I had not informed Andy of my step-by-step process due to my uncertainty of how it would pan out, and he did not know my innermost thoughts as they related to this phase of my search. Because I had been mistaken about Omar, I did not tell Andy the details of my next play. Nevertheless, that "yay" was hurtful, and as I watched him exit the room on his way to run an errand that could have waited five more damn minutes, I was pissed.

After Andy left, I quickly got a lump of rejection in my throat and called my friend Tammie. Tammie and Andy had a great relationship as they held executive titles in large companies and engaged in many conversations surrounding their occupations. Tammie calmed me down and explained why she thought Andy reacted in the way he did toward me. She eventually convinced me not to open the letter alone. She told me to bring it to her home in Baltimore, Maryland, since I already had plans to go there for the weekend. We would also be together with our friend Barbara. Tammie believed this news was way too important, and I needed support from my close girlfriends when what was in the envelope was revealed.

After we hung up, I swallowed my pride and placed the recently delivered and unopened envelope in my purse. I also did not utter another word to Andy for the rest of the day. The weekend would soon be here, and since I waited a long time for this information to arrive, another few days would not make a difference.

I also called my daughter, Jordyne, and discussed what happened earlier that day. She apologized for her father's reaction and told me how excited she was for me to get closer to finding out my truth. We spoke for about a half hour, and our conversation validated me for being upset with Andy.

Other things were able to occupy my mind and keep it off of the opening of my birth certificate. I had recently been appointed the chairman of a large public meeting that was to occur during the upcoming North Atlantic Regional Conference of my beloved Alpha Kappa Alpha Sorority, Inc. The event was planned for the evening of March 9, 2023, at the Pennsylvania Convention Center. My nerves were already high because there were an anticipated 5,000 guests, including some state senators and representatives plus local celebrities, to complicate matters for my stress level. Therefore, I threw myself into completing the planning for that event instead of dwelling on what was inside my purse.

March 5th finally arrived, and I was packed and off to Baltimore to visit my girlfriends Tammie and Barbara. The final check to see if my letter was included in my belongings was complete, and off I went. Upon arrival at Tammie's home, we relaxed and waited for Barbara to arrive at the Baltimore/Washington airport. Then, the two of us left to pick her up. Tammie made a great dinner of crab cakes, baked potatoes, and salad, which we happily devoured.

After a while, Tammie looked at me and asked, "Gia, are you ready to open the letter?"

"Yes, I am," I replied, retrieving it from my purse. Everyone gathered around the island in Tammie's kitchen as I opened it.

Dear Customer:
Recently, you wrote the Louisiana Center for Records
and Statistics in New Orleans and placed an order for
one or more vital records. Your order is enclosed
herewith.
Pursuant to LA R.S. 40:73, enclosed you will find a copy
of the certificate requested.
It was a pleasure serving you. If we may be of further
assistance, please contact us.

I took a deep breath and looked at the enclosure. It was a certificate of live birth. The birth number was identical to the one on the only birth certificate I had known, the one given to my adoptive parents. That was how the office could trace the source of the original one issued. I read it aloud to Tammie and Barbara as I inspected it.

My eyes went directly to my birth name.

"My name was Shevonne Marie Franklin!"

I was born on October 2, 1965, at 2:42 PM at the U.S. Public Health Service Hospital in New Orleans, Louisiana, Orleans County. My mother's street address was provided, but the father's name and information were left blank. The rest of the information listed for her was her name, Patricia Ann Franklin, age 16, and she was from Kenner, Louisiana. It also had my mother's signature. It also revealed that the number of children living at the time of birth was none, and no miscarriages were listed.

I was so relieved that my name was indeed Shevonne Marie. I don't recall Tina mentioning any last name of Franklin to me, but when I spoke to Audrey Bean, I remembered her theory that my father must have been one of the seven Franklin men. This was a match, and she must be correct. I ran my finger repeatedly over my mother's signature because it was the first real thing I ever had of hers, and I kept staring at the document with a sense of calm.

I now knew who my biological mother was, and it was time to get cracking.

Tammie exclaimed, "And I got it all on tape!"

I looked up at her and replied, "I did not know you were taping me."

"I think this moment was far too important for us not to record it," she answered. And with that, she texted me a copy of the recording.

I wasn't the only one waiting for the results. Stephanie was anticipating my call once the letter was opened. I shared the information with her on speakerphone as I introduced her to my friends. Barbara and Stephanie then collaborated, leaving both to bang away on their respective keyboards to discover how everything connected. Together, they searched the census records, and I looked up things using Google. After a while, we retired for the evening, and I promised to reach out to Cousin Audrey soon with the news. My family tree was about to grow!

After enjoying the remainder of my time with Tammie and Barbara and returning home, I decided to call Cousin Audrey before resuming my duties with the upcoming conference. There were better times for this to come to a head. Where should my loyalties lie? Ugh, this was so difficult!

Andy also returned home that evening from his workday in New York City. I decided not to mention my new revelations to him because I felt he did not deserve to know. You guessed it, I was still angry with him. As he entered, he came up behind me as I sat at the kitchen counter, leaned over, and kissed me on the cheek. I looked up at him and noticed he was holding a beautiful bouquet, which he then handed to me, saying, "I am so sorry for how I acted the other day when you were trying to share your news. I was not aware how close you were to finding your family."

I quickly accepted his apology and asked, "Who called you, Jordyne?"

"No, Tammie," he said.

My girl Tammie had my back. She called Andy to inform him of the monumental things occurring lately with my search and that she did not want him to miss out on this moment. She had shared the video she took of me opening the birth certificate with him, and he admitted he had watched it. Tammie's quick thinking gave my husband and daughters a front seat to my essential, life-changing news.

After a few minutes of speaking with Andy, I picked up the phone and called Audrey.

"Hi, Audrey! Well, I have some news. I finally received my original birth certificate, and my mother's name was Patricia Ann Franklin. Does her name ring a bell with you?"

Audrey paused for a few seconds as she thought and then exclaimed, "I've got it! I know how we are connected!"

She went on to tell me that she remembered a story that was told to her many years ago about a scandal in Baton Rouge, Louisiana, when she was growing up. The seven Franklin boys also had two sisters, Ruby and Thelma. Thelma never married. However, Ruby married Leonard Martin Sr. (Pudding was his nickname). That would have made Leonard Martin Sr. Patricia's uncle through marriage. Leonard, age 39, was considerably older than Patricia as she was only 15 years old when he must have impregnated her with me. There is no way to know if this was a violent, one-time event or if Patricia was molested by Leonard more than once, but the fact remains that Leonard Martin Sr. was the man who sired me. To give him the name of father would not happen. He did nothing to be one to me except donate his sperm to add to the egg from which I grew. These things occurred frequently back then, as they still do today.

Audrey continued telling me that Patricia was her first cousin and the daughter of Joseph Franklin, who was Audrey's uncle. That made me Audrey's second cousin, which explained the "once removed" on the Ancestry DNA record. Instead of being the daughter of a Franklin sibling, I was the granddaughter of Joseph Franklin.

Ruby and Leonard never had children of their own. However, Leonard had other children from previous relationships. This pregnancy put a significant strain on the Franklin family as Patricia's father, Joseph, was so hurt that his only daughter was essentially raped by a man who was an authority figure to her, and she should have been able to trust him. The family begged Ruby to divorce Leonard for doing what he did to Patricia, but Ruby refused to do so. Instead, Ruby and Leonard would remain married until death parted them. Leonard died in 1990, while Ruby died in 2007.

Audrey was unaware of any children Patricia may have had as they were not close in age. Audrey also moved to California many years ago and had not stayed in touch. She did confirm that Patricia was deceased, and she thought that her complications with diabetes were the reason she passed away. Audrey urged me to call her first cousin, Farien Franklin Christian, daughter of Willie Franklin, who could tell me more about my mother because she knew her better. In closing, Audrey wished me well, gave me Farien's phone number, and we hung up.

I took a deep breath and gathered my thoughts about the news I just heard from Audrey. Because of the age difference between my mother and father from the non-identifying information I had received many years ago, the probability that I was the product of a non-conventional conception was now confirmed. A feeling of deep sadness washed over me as I thought about the terrible journey my mother went through as a young girl. What went through her mind while she was carrying me? No wonder she gave me away and could not think of raising me. I would be that constant reminder of that sad time in her life. I felt sick to my stomach.

After a few minutes of reflection and self-pity, I called Farien. She was warm and friendly as I told her who I was and informed her of my conversation with her cousin Audrey. Farien shared that she attended my mother's funeral and had pictures of her to share with me, as well as pictures of the man who sired me. She told me that she wanted to assist me in putting the pieces together and that Patricia did have other children.

Wow, that meant that I had some brothers and sisters! How exciting. I wondered if I could find them.

Farien and I vowed to stay in touch, and she told me that she would gather the pieces and items to share with me. I thanked her profusely, and we ended our long conversation. I quickly added Farien's information to my address book and sent her a follow-up text message thanking her for speaking with me.

She replied, "You are welcome. What is your mailing address? I will mail you this obituary and anything I have."

I answered her eagerly and sent her my headshot so she could put a face with my name.

Farien responded, "How beautiful you are and I think you look just like Patricia."

"Aww. Thank you."

My cell phone kept dinging with more messages from Farien. One of those texts included a picture of a beautiful woman with the message, "Look at the nose and the mouth area."

My heart stopped as I realized this was a picture of my mother, Patricia. It was the first picture that I would ever lock eyes with. I felt a sense of calm.

I knew this was finally the truth, and there was no doubt that it was correct. At this moment in time, I finally culminated all those years of mistakes and redirection.

Farien kept texting me items, including my mother's funeral celebration program, Ruby's funeral program, Ruby and Leonard's wedding photos, and information on a home that Ruby and Leonard owned in Baton Rouge that went into their estate after Ruby passed away.

There were no living heirs to whom the property could be accessed. However, Leonard knew he had a daughter – ME - whom he talked about for the remainder of his life. Without knowing my whereabouts or where to begin looking for me, someone purchased the home in 2022 by buying the tax lien for a few thousand, fixed it up, and sold it for $52,300.

Once again, I connected with Stephanie to fill her in on my conversations and shared my pictures. Given the new information I had secured, Stephanie got to work quickly and resumed her detective work. Within an hour, I received messages from Stephanie with the obituaries of Leonard, Ruby, Patricia, and Joseph, among other family members.

I could not believe that I had finally discovered I had a slew of blood relatives... aunts, uncles, and cousins. I reviewed the information Stephanie sent with all the obituaries to find any new revelations.

Leonard Martin, Sr. "Pudding" of Baton Rouge, died on Friday, November 23, 1990. He was 64. He was survived by his wife, Cloverine "Ruby" Franklin Martin, two daughters, a son, Leonard Martin, Jr., and three sisters. His occupation was listed as a "Paper Hanger." This made sense to me because of the non-identifying information I had received many years ago from the adoption agency, and his occupation was listed as a painter. Most painters also hung wallpaper—a match.

Cloverine "Ruby" Martin died on Friday, July 13, 2007. She was 73. She was preceded in death by her parents, husband, Leonard Martin Sr, a stepson, a sister (Thelma), and six brothers, John, Willie, Daniel, Charlie, James, and Perry Franklin.

Joseph Franklin of Baton Rouge, my grandfather, died on May 5, 2017. He was a WWII Navy Veteran who survived the Port Chicago disaster in 1944. One son and four grandchildren survived him.

Patricia Blackston entered eternal rest on Friday, August 20, 2010. She was 61. Beloved daughter of Joseph and the late Bessie Franklin. Loving wife of Louis Blackston, Sr., Mother of Nicole Fountain, Louis Blackston, Derrick Blackston, and Aprile Kenney. She was survived by many grandchildren, nieces, nephews, cousins, and other relatives and friends.

I gathered the names of her children - my siblings. On the original announcement, my baby sister, Aprile, was omitted, so at the time, I feverishly started searching on Facebook for Louis Blackston Jr., Nicole Blackston-

Fountain, and Derrick Blackston. Stephanie had already done her research and texted me that they were all on Facebook and that I should try to reach out to them.

A flurry of questions once again popped into my mind. Which one should I contact first? Based on each of their activities and carefully weighing my options, I finally decided to reach out to my sister, Nicole, because she appeared to interact more frequently on Facebook than Derrick and Louis.

Meanwhile, March 9th was quickly approaching, and my conference was gearing up. I was going to have to write a letter to her and wait for her reply while I was getting through my big event! This was not a convenient time, but I couldn't wait. I wanted us to connect because time was of the essence! I was just going to have to multitask if I was going to strike gold.

Stephanie had also coached me not to "beat around the bush" with Nicole and just to be direct in telling her who I was.

Rip the Band-Aid off!

I had my marching orders and charged ahead.

Tuesday, March 7, 2023, 9:58 PM. Me:
Hi Nicole, are you the daughter of Patricia
Ann Franklin Blackston? If so, I think I am
your half-sister. I am the first child of
Patricia. She had me at 16 and gave me up
for adoption in New Orleans. I would like to
talk because I never had actual blood
relatives and would like to get to know you
and my half-brothers. You can call me if you
would like. I am just learning this connection
after years of searching for her. My only
regret is that I am too late to meet her. I am
57 years old.

I nervously awaited her reply. I also needed to finish preparing for the big event my sorority was holding. That was my focus, as a distraction from my anxiety.

A whole day and a half later and on the afternoon of my colossal event, I received a message notification:

Thursday, March 9, 2023, 12:40 PM. Nicole:
Hi, yes, I am. I don't know anything about
this. I don't believe this because of the type
of mother I had. She would have been
looking for you instead of you looking for
her. I'm sorry if there's some truth to this,
but as of now, I'm gonna leave the past in
the past. I can only go off the mother that I
know. The mom, I know, would have told us
about you at some point. We would have
helped her find you. She's dead and gone
now, so it's no need to discuss this. I hope
you have a nice life. Sorry.

Oh no! I scared her, and now she was turning her back on me. She did not want to have anything to do with me. More questions whirled through my head. How should I respond now? Should I respond? She's the only viable next step I can think of, so I decided to take the softer, nonthreatening approach so I would not seem pushy. I was just excited to find someone who could be my sister.

Me:
Ok, I understand. I did not mean any harm. I was just happy to discover the truth after many years, but I am at peace and have had a wonderful life.

Best wishes.

I attached a picture of myself so Nicole could see what I looked like, hoping she would soften. I realized that I came on strong and scared her.

Tammie also pointed out that I needed to understand that I had just blown up her world and should back off somewhat so she could process the situation.

Nicole responded kindly.

I just want to let you know you are a beautiful lady, and if I want to discuss further, I'll reach out.

Did my new approach work? Nicole seemed to leave the door open for a possible conversation. Maybe I should let her know I have some proof so she doesn't think I'm trying to pull something cruel on her through the internet.

Me
Ok. Just so you know, I have my official birth certificate.

Nicole
Ok.

Now, it was time for me to focus on the pending event that I was to lead, so I let go of all of these thoughts and started to focus on the details of the evening. Andy had gone to the convention center with me and helped me put things in place so things would go according to schedule. Having him by my side helped calm my nerves. Once the event went off without a hitch and I returned to my room in the late evening, I realized I had received another message from Nicole. I informed Tammie that the message was received, and we sat down to tend to it.

Thursday, March 9, 2023, 6:17 PM. Nicole:
Hey, it's me again. I've been thinking of you ever since we messaged each other. I'm not ready to close the door. I talked to my sister and I think it's some things we need to talk about. So can you please send me your number and when I get a chance I'll call you. I'm at work right now, but I can't get you off my mind. Thanks.

OMG, yes! There was another way to reach Nicole. She can't get me off of her mind. Did she see any resemblance between me and Patricia? Instead of answering right then, Tammie and I decided to think about my next move and how I could approach Nicole so she was not scared off again.

The following day, I answered her.

Friday, March 10, 2023, 7:32 AM. Me:
Hi Nicole, this is my number. Nicole, I am excited to speak with you. However, I understand how difficult and shocking this must be for you, so you have my number, and when you're ready, I pray that you reach out to me so we can connect. I've waited 57 years for this moment and if I have to wait a little longer, it will be worth it to speak with you. I am not looking for anything other than getting to know my biological family.

She answered in a few hours.

Friday, March 10, 2023, 9:48 AM. Nicole:
Good morning. Yes, this is really hard for me. I have so many questions. But I'm willing to have the conversation. I'm about to get ready to go to work, but I'll have time tomorrow. So, hopefully, I can get up the courage to give you a call. Thanks for answering me. Talk to you soon.

I was so relieved. There was a new opportunity pending. Thank God I brought my original birth certificate and paperwork to the hotel, so if Nicole needed proof after our conversation, proof she would get.

That day was the first official day of the conference, so I went on and attended the meetings; all the while, I was thinking about Nicole and how our conversation would go the next day.

Before I knew it, Saturday arrived. It was possibly the day I would finally speak to my sister! I needed to have my phone handy constantly just in case.

That morning was filled with educational meetings, so I decided to move my day along as planned. We had a more significant sorority meeting later that afternoon while I waited to receive a call from her.

I was stationed within the first two rows of a vast auditorium, listening intently to what the leaders and presenters were saying with my phone silenced. During one of the pauses as speakers were changing, I saw that I had missed a call at 3:29 PM from someone with a 504 area code. I thought it odd that I did not feel my phone vibrate. I quickly looked at the transcribed voicemail message.

"Hi, Gia. This is Nicole. Could you call me when you get this message? Thank you."

She left her phone number for me. What was I going to do? By now, the meeting was in full force, so I could only text her.

Saturday, March 11, 2023 at 3:52 PM. Me:
Hi. Sorry I missed your call, but I am in a meeting. What would be a good time to call you back? I will be free at 5:30 or 4:30 your time.

Nicole:
OK, I'm here all day. Anytime is OK.

Me:
I'll call you in 30 minutes. This is too important to me. I will leave and go back to my room and call you. This meeting can wait!

Nicole:
Finish your meeting. I'll be here. I promise it's gonna happen.

I sat for another few minutes and shared my news with my good friend Yolanda, who was sitting beside me. Yolanda asked me what I was going to do.

My mind started racing. What was my escape route? I waited for my friend, Arla, to complete her presentation, quickly jumped up and said goodbye to Yolanda, and then made my way to the exit door, which seemed like it took an eternity to reach because of the size of the room.

As I returned to my hotel room, my heart started racing a mile a minute. I did not want to mess this up. What was I going to say? How was I going to tell it? UGH, I wanted to vomit!

Once I reached my room, I threw my things down on the bed. I grabbed my paperwork to have it handy during the call and shook my arms nervously to release some tension, or so I hoped. I even jumped up and down before saying a prayer and calling.

Nicole answered, "You just couldn't wait, could you?"

"No, I couldn't! I needed to talk to you because I have a big gala tonight, and if I waited until the meeting was over, our conversation would be rushed because I had to prepare for that."

Nicole laughed and said, "Alright."

I quickly filled her in on all the information I had gathered and how I concluded that we were sisters and shared the same mother. I also told her about the unfortunate circumstances around my conception, which was difficult.

In spite of this, our conversation was so easy, and we got along like we had known each other for the longest time. Nicole explained to me how hard it was to lose her mother, and she wanted this to be true because if it was, she felt like she would be getting a small piece of her mother back through me.

I thought that was the sweetest thing she could have said to me and quickly offered to send her a copy of my original birth certificate via text message right after we hung up. I told Nicole I was not looking for anything more than getting to know her and my brothers and finally being at peace with the truth. Nicole told me that there was a younger sister named Aprile. They all had the same father, who was Patricia Ann's husband until the day she passed away.

Nicole did not have to take my word for it, and I also wanted there to be no mistake after what I experienced with Omar. I asked her to allow me to purchase the Ancestry DNA kit so she could take it and verify the information herself. I was that certain.

I then asked Nicole what made her change her mind about speaking with me. She admitted that she initially thought it was a hoax, but after speaking with her son, Lavelis, Jr., and her youngest sister, Aprile, they also wanted to find out the truth. Therefore, Nicole agreed to take the test.

Nicole told me that she and her son were traveling to Las Vegas soon to celebrate his twenty-first birthday, so time was of the essence. I was so relieved that I gathered Nicole's mailing information to get to work on that front. We spoke effortlessly for about two hours before hanging up, almost forgetting I had a gala to get to that evening. Once our conversation ended, I ordered Nicole's kit so she could send her sample in before she left for her trip.

Nicole wasn't the only one with travel plans. Tammie and I would also be leaving for Italy later that month, overlapping some days Nicole and her son would be in Vegas. Once I completed the order, I texted Nicole to inform her that I would send her the tracking information as soon as I received it so she could be aware of its arrival. I also remembered to text her a picture of my original birth certificate so she could inspect it herself. Nicole wished me an enjoyable evening and probably could tell I was a bundle of nerves by then. I also let Nicole know that when I returned home the following evening, I would send her a copy of my re-issued birth certificate with my adopted name so she could see that the birth numbers were identical, further proof I was who I said I was.

As promised, I gathered myself after sending the text with a picture of my original birth certificate. I got ready for the big gala that evening, feeling hopeful and anticipating what was to come.

"We must accept finite disappointment but never lose infinite hope." — Martin Luther King, Jr

---

CHAPTER 14

COULD THE PUZZLE PIECES BE STARTING TO FIT?

> Hey, that's her handwriting on that birth certificate.

I was at the Gala when I glanced at my phone and saw the text message from Nicole.

She validated that Patricia's signature was on my original birth certificate.

I knew then that Nicole was convinced I was her sister, and the DNA results were just a formality. There was no way I could know Patricia's signature, so her acknowledgment made me know everything was true for us.

Over the next days, I shared photos of my family and daily messages with Nicole.

Nicole then sent me a message.

> I want to see the man that fathered you. I don't want to call him your father. Don't know if I should look at him.

I felt terrible that Nicole had realized that Patricia was

possibly hurt by this man who was supposed to be a family friend and relative through marriage. It left a knot in the pit of my stomach. I answered,

Not necessary right now. Step by step.

Ok, I'll listen to you.

Nicole then sent two pink heart emojis.

On March 13th, I texted Nicole the video of me opening up my birth certificate at Tammie's house. She replied to let me know that it brought her to tears while viewing it.

Over the next few weeks, Nicole and I exchanged daily text messages. One of the questions I asked her was whether her father knew that Patricia had a child before they met. She did not think he knew.

That following Monday, Nicole received the Ancestry DNA kit in time to deposit her sample and mail it off before leaving for Las Vegas. Tammie and I would also be going to Italy the following day, so this was an excellent time for it to arrive.

Ancestry sent Nicole a message on March 24th informing her that her DNA kit had been received. So we were off to participate in the waiting game again, but at least we were both traveling, and that would occupy our minds for a little while. This sample result would take about five weeks to appear.

In the meantime, I had conversations with Stephanie about the probability of the DNA match coming out correctly, primarily because of what had happened with Omar. Would the same thing happen with Nicole? Could I bear another disappointment?

Stephanie reassured me that this time, it would be a

match. She was 100% sure. Stephanie herself had half-siblings, so I had the idea to ask her what percentage of DNA they shared so I could set the expectation for Nicole. That way, she would not have any doubts once the results came back. Stephanie said that half-siblings usually test around 25%. I then shared this information with Nicole.

Over the next few weeks, Nicole and I became attached, texting back and forth daily. However, I was reluctant to ask if she told the brothers about me. Aprile knew about me, but she never called me, so I was hesitant to ask Nicole for her number. Perhaps Nicole wanted to wait for confirmation that we were a match before she let the others speak with me.

Before Nicole's DNA results came back, I grew increasingly confident that we would be confirmed as a match. I wanted to plan a trip to New Orleans to meet my newly discovered family. Nicole told me that Aprile usually visits New Orleans for a few weeks during June every year and that their church was planning its 100th anniversary to be held on the first Sunday in June.

Tammie and Barbara told me they wanted to accompany me because Andy and our daughters could not come to New Orleans due to their own school and work schedules. They also did not want me to go alone. Therefore, with the utmost faith, on Friday, April 14th, we all purchased our plane tickets, secured our hotel, and rented our car in anticipation of this big reunion. I would have a chance to meet all four of my siblings at once. We were so excited.

"And whatever you ask in prayer, you will receive if you have faith." - Matthew 21:2

Gia opening her birth certificate

CHAPTER 15
OMG, HALLELUJAH!

My attention was back to sorority business as usual, with my sorority chapter meeting the next day, on Saturday, April 15th. At the end of the meeting, I noticed Stephanie had tried to call me, but since I kept my phone silenced during the sessions, I missed the call.

She texted me to look at my Ancestry account, so I quickly pulled it up on my laptop. I had a new match!

Nicole Blackston-Fountain was a 26% match for me!

This confirmed it. Nicole was my sister! It was almost as though I willed the results to come through by cementing my plans to travel to New Orleans. My heart started racing, and all I could do was turn around and share my news with Gina, my sorority sister, sitting directly behind me. I tried to collect myself because I had not shared my story with everyone in the room, but Gina knew my story, so she was there for me. Of course, I quickly texted Stephanie to tell her I received the great news. I also texted Nicole, who was at work.

Confirmed! WE ARE SISTERS!

Nicole replied.

You got the results?

YUP. THEY ARE POSTED. I just checked
like I do every day.

Oh, Lord. I'm at work, and my heart has
dropped.

Here look!

I sent Nicole a screenshot of the results.

OMG, I am so happy!!!!!!! I am going to call
you when I get off.

After the meeting, I went out to celebrate a birthday, and I could now share my news with my sorority sisters about my real sisters and brothers. Everyone was so happy for me; I needed the comfort.

Later that evening, Nicole and I were finally able to talk as sisters for the first time. She was excited that everything worked out as we had hoped. Nicole told me that she planned to tell our brothers about me and that I planned to visit now that everything was confirmed. They all resided in New Orleans, except Aprile. I could hear Lavelis, Jr., Nicole's son, enter the room. Everyone calls him Tuttie, especially family, which I guess means me now. Aprile called Tuttie on his phone, as she does almost daily, and was now on speakerphone. She said, "Hey, Gia, it's Aprile." I could hear her voice for the first time and knew she was my sister. It was beautiful to confirm this and discover I had two sisters and two brothers. My life was blooming, and my family tree was growing beyond my wildest dreams!

With the confirmation of the test results, the time had now come to tell Omar of my new discoveries and real siblings. As we spoke about our feelings towards one another over the past ten years, we decided to continue to keep in touch and maintain our relationship.

I informed him of my impending trip to New Orleans. We mutually agreed to meet in person during my time there, and I felt really great about his reaction to my new developments. As we hung up, he said, "Gia, you will always be my big Sis."

It warmed my heart, and I was very relieved.

"If you lose faith, you lose all." — Eleanor Roosevelt

CHAPTER 16

ANTICIPATION

Once we had confirmed the DNA was a match, Tammie, Barbara, and I solidified our plans to visit my relatives in New Orleans. Once again, time seemed to pass slowly as we looked forward to our trip. Luckily, there were other items to occupy me and take my mind off of things. I would exchange daily text messages and pictures of my family with my sisters and sometimes participate in FaceTime calls so we could see each other in real-time. My family also spent time on FaceTime meetings with their families and vice versa. We enjoyed getting to know each other.

During our cherished "Sissy Poo call," Nicole opened up about her husband, Lavelis, Sr., explaining his struggle with a diagnosis of depression, which has impacted his daily life and interaction with family. She shared her efforts to support him and their challenges as a couple. Additionally, Nicole and I discussed the strained relationship between our brothers, Louis Jr. and Derrick, emphasizing the importance of family unity. Throughout our conversations, the bond between Nicole and me strengthened, providing a space for open, heartfelt discussions about our lives and the hurdles we encounter, highlighting the power of family support and understanding in navigating life's challenges.

I told my siblings I was not coming to "fix" the family dynamics that were in motion before I entered the picture. However, I wanted a picture of the five of us all together. They told me we could work on achieving this feat, but made no promises on the outcome.

While we continued to visit via FaceTime, Nicole smiled and declared, "I never had a big sister I could confide in!"

It was almost like this sense of relief washed over her, and she could finally breathe now that she had gotten it all out and it was no longer a secret to me.

Truthfully, it made me feel honored that my sisters and I seemed to move ever so quickly into devoted and trusted family members with whom we could share some of our innermost thoughts and the problematic things we were living with daily—share our true selves in the raw. These items warranted prayers toward healing.

I shared that Andy's mother, Linnette, who is 95, has lived with us for the last several years, and I am now her caregiver, which presents many challenges for me because of my busy and active schedule. As she ages, more medical issues have cropped up, and although I love her dearly, it infringes on my ability to move freely about my life as I was accustomed to. Having to get her to many doctor visits and physical therapy appointments is very nerve-racking, especially since her mobility has declined. My perpetual fear of arriving late is a constant. No matter what, I know this is the best place for her, and I will be blessed. I keep telling myself that I will have no regrets once she closes her eyes for the last time, pushing me to have more patience.

I'm not going to lie... I am far from perfecting my patience, but I always strive towards it!

My brother-in-law and his wife had agreed to keep Linnette from the middle of May through June because Andy and I would celebrate our 35th wedding anniversary that May on his native island of Jamaica before my girlfriends and I were scheduled to leave for New Orleans for our big adventure.

Each day in Jamaica, my siblings and I communicated, and I sent them pictures of me enjoying the time with Andy. Andy and I discussed what awaited me and how my life would change to incorporate my extended family—the calm before the frenzy was needed and welcomed as I caught up on much-needed rest.

While on vacation, I also reached out to Omar to let him know that I would be visiting NOLA and wanted to meet him and have dinner on the evening of May 31st, the first night of my arrival. I made dinner reservations at the Red Fish Grill on Bourbon Street in the French Quarter, blocks from the Residence Inn where we would stay. Omar was sent the reservation in advance, and I looked forward to fulfilling my promise to continue our relationship as friends instead of siblings. This way, he would not have to "lose" his Big Sis.

After we returned from Jamaica, I had one day to unpack, grab my pre-packed suitcase for New Orleans, and drive to Tammie's home in Baltimore since we were flying out of BWI. The buildup of anticipation was almost unbearable.

I kept my sisters informed of my every move, but they knew where I was at every step of my journey because we had all decided to share our respective locations before I left for Jamaica.

They would text me with messages like, "I can see you at the airport!" which let me know they were just as excited as I was. It was sort of like *Where's Waldo*? I wondered if they thought I was "catfishing" them and somehow was not a real person.

We had grown closer over the last several weeks as we gathered and shared information about each other's lives, and our meeting time was finally near.

You and
Nicole Blackston-Fountain

Half sister | Maternal side ⓘ

26% shared DNA. 1,804 cM across 50 segments

Message   Edit Relationship

CHAPTER 17
WOOSAH!

When I landed in New Orleans, I sent Nicole and Aprile a message telling them I had successfully landed, picked up the rental minivan, and waited for Barbara to arrive. Tammie was to come later that night because one of her dear friend's mother had passed away, and she had to attend the funeral that same day, making her need to change her flight. Tammie was hell-bent on not missing out on our initial meet and greet. After all, Tammie and Barbara were my paparazzi and security detail in tow.

Barbara and I walked to Red Fish to meet Omar for our six o'clock reservation. I was a little nervous because we were meeting for the first time. Since he had not confirmed or replied to my text message with the reservation details, I was unsure if he would show up. However, I followed up with a message saying I was looking forward to meeting him.

I asked Barbara to accompany me since I felt uneasy, and in case he did not show, I could enjoy a good dinner with my girlfriend instead. If he did show, I would have her there for moral support. Barbara and I arrived on time, but Omar did not show, nor did he text me or call me with his apology. Therefore, as girlfriends always do, Barbara and I enjoyed a lovely dinner consisting of specialty cocktails, alligator boudin balls, Louisiana shrimp and grits, and wood-grilled swordfish. We were sated and happy as could be. Afterward, we walked up and down Bourbon Street while the bars started to come alive and the street filled up with tourists before returning to our hotel to wait for Tammie's late-night arrival.

I was hurt that Omar did not reach out to me and stood me up. Who does that? If he had second thoughts, all he had to do was tell me. I would have understood. Late that same night at 11:47 PM, my phone dinged. It was a message from Omar.

> Hi, Gia; sorry I didn't get back to you. I just had car trouble today. Got it fixed, but it's still acting up so I have to bring it back to the shop tomorrow morning, but I'll FaceTime you tomorrow so you can see me, but I'm so sorry.

What the heck! If he had car trouble, he had my cell phone number and could have called before the designated time to inform me of the situation. He did not know if I was sitting there at Red Fish all alone or what. Now he waited until almost midnight to reach out to me?! I was livid and decided not to reply that evening.

I texted his cousin, Daphne, whom I had been communicating with, to complain, and she was upset because of what happened with him. She said that perhaps he was heartbroken that I was not his sister after all. I told her that I could understand that, but it was an honest mistake, and I wanted to ensure that maintaining a friendship with him was my goal to keep him from feeling that total void.

The time had now come to retrieve Tammie from the airport and bring her back to the hotel so the festivities could start the following day.

Aprile and her husband Lawrence, and their two daughters, Makaylah and Lana, dropped their collie dog, Nola, off at the groomers, where they would kennel her periodically. The following day, they hit the road towards New Orleans. It was June 1, 2023, and the drive for them to meet us was about five hours.

Nicole and I were constantly informed where they were. While we waited for their arrival, Tammie, Barbara, and I hit the streets of the French Quarter in search of the coveted Cafe du Monde flagship location to partake in beignets and coffee, plus get a little boutique shopping on and people-watching until I would finally meet my family. The air was filled with gleeful anticipation of what the day would hold.

We returned to our hotel room to freshen up, rest, and await the word that the coast was clear to come over so we could have our much-anticipated special moment. I finally got the text from Aprile around 5:46 PM on June 1st.

You ready, Sis?

I replied,

Been ready!

Ok, we are, too. C'mon!

Aprile texted.

I asked Barbara to drive because I was too nervous to do so, and off we went to Nicole's home to meet my siblings.

Nicole lived around two miles from the French Quarter, so the commute was short. As we drove up and parked at the house, my heart was doing backflips. Tammie and Barbara jumped out ahead of me to get in place to film the meeting and to take pictures. I stayed back and said a prayer that everything would go well.

As I exited the van, I shook my arms at my side, "Woosah, woosah." Yes, this was a woosah moment, as Dr. Iyanla Vanzant had referred to it.... a way to take a deep breath and refuse to act on the impulse of anger. Mine was not the impulse of anger, just extreme nervousness.

As people gathered in the front yard, I crossed the street and approached the house. My niece, Lana, Aprile's youngest daughter, was the first person I came to because she was outside already. I greeted and embraced her as the others filed out. Once I turned around, I locked eyes with Nicole, followed by Aprile. We hugged, started tearing up, and did not want to let go.

Amid our bonding, our brother Louis emerged from inside the house and started to make his way to us as we were still hugging with the announcement, "Here I come to meet my sister!"

I took Nicole and Aprile individually and embraced them to give them one-on-one time.

While I hugged Nicole, teary-eyed, Aprile exclaimed, "She looks like Mama!"

Nicole replied, "Sure do" In her thick New Orleans accent.

Louis said, "Y'all let her go. I want some hugs, too."

Aprile laughed and greedily responded to him, "You wait!"

After I finished with Nicole, I hugged Aprile while she wept in my arms.

Finally, Louis would receive his long-awaited hug from me.

As I went in for my hug with Louis, Nicole showed her sibling love for him by exclaiming and jokingly dubbing him, "The disgusting one of the crew."

Louis and I embraced as he said, "This is the best one right here! This is the one you're gonna love the most right here!" He kissed me on the cheek, looked into my eyes, and said, "You do look like her."

To hear this from their lips at that moment that I resembled our mother, Patricia, nearly made my knees buckle.

"We may encounter many defeats, but we must not be defeated. It may even be necessary to encounter the defeat so that we can know who we are." - Maya Angelou

---

CHAPTER 18
THE GIFTS

I could hear Aprile behind me saying, "Oh my gosh, she looks like Mama!"

Louis agreed and said, "Don't she, though?"

Then Nicole added, "She looks like Papa Joe."

Papa Joe was our late grandfather and Patricia's father. Aprile and Louis agreed aloud, "She looks like him, too."

I greeted my other niece, Makaylah, my nephew Tuttie, and my brother-in-law, Lawrence who said, "It is nice to finally meet you in person."

Tammie and Barbara were also introduced to everyone, although I admit I was caught up connecting with my found family.

I have often heard a faint question of curiosity when strangers believed I reminded them of someone, but this was different. Their confirmation hit stronger than the test results I'd focused on for the last few months. It was like my family had seen our mother's ghost. They thought it was crazy how much we resembled each other as we stood there briefly and talked.

I said to them, wondering why they had this reaction, "You have seen me on FaceTime."

Nicole described it as "scary" how much I looked like our mother.

Aprile agreed, "It is so different over the phone and Facebook. You look even more like her. You are even shaped like her!!"

Louis told me about his two sons and daughter, giving me more auntie love to spread around, but they could not come in from Dallas to meet me. He said he was trying to fly them in for the special occasion.

Nicole retrieved her next-door neighbors, whom she told about me, and returned with them in tow. We took additional pictures together and then went inside to continue our visit.

Soon after, Louis and Lawrence went out to get everyone dinner while we assembled in the home's central area. Nicole's husband, Lavelis Sr., was inside, and I greeted him and his mother, Ms. Ruth, as I entered. Lavelis Sr. seemed to be waiting for me at the door, looking dressed for the occasion, which pleased me immensely, knowing how much he had been going through each day.

We all took seats around the room and started to exchange the gifts we brought for each other. I was the first receiver. My niece Lana painted a cute AKA design on a canvas, complete with pearls, one of our sorority signatures. She had shared the painting with me on one of our Sissy Poo FaceTime calls one evening, and I thought it was so sweet of her to spend time preparing it for me. Now, it was finally mine, and I knew where it would hang in my office at home. My other gifts included a pink and green purse tassel from Aprile. Nicole presented me with a lovely pink and green glass beaded bracelet made by a lady that she and Aprile regularly purchased from for themselves.

I brought gifts for Makaylah, Lana and Tuttie and I doled them out. They each took turns opening them and reading their cards aloud. I had gifted them each with a gift card and told Lana I wanted her to purchase more art supplies. Tuttie was instructed to buy something he loved and Makaylah was to get her glam beauty products for herself. One thing we discovered during one of our many pre-meet conversations was that Makaylah and Jordyne were both social workers. Another similarity shared between our families!

Now it was my turn to finally make my presentations to my newest and dearest Sissy Poos. I instructed Nicole to sit to my right and Aprile to sit to my left on the couch.

Nicole was giddy with anticipation, exclaiming, "The Poos. The Poos!"

Aprile pleaded, "Don't make me cry again!"

They both sat down as instructed and started opening their cards. Nicole started to read, "Siblings Reunited....."

I told her to look at the front of the card carefully. That is when she noticed they were custom cards that I created for them. On the front was artwork where five different colored, handprints of different sizes bore the names of the five siblings, ranging from largest to smallest. My name was on the largest one, and the rest were on the descending age and size, depicting the order of all of us. At the base of all the hands in a circular pattern was a pink heart with Mom on it.

Aprile immediately burst into tears and said, "Really, I said I did not want to cry!"

I put a collage on the interior of the card. The first picture, on the top left, was a picture of our mother, which all her family cherished. Next to that one on the top right was a picture of me at age one; under the picture of our mother was a picture of me at age sixteen, and on the bottom right was a recent photo of me. The picture of Patricia and the one directly below her of me at sixteen was so eerie because it looked as if we were the same person. We had the same hair and expression on our faces, me appearing as the younger version of her. No one could deny the fact that I was her daughter.

As Nicole opened her card for the first time, she immediately tossed it up as if it were on fire and started to rock back and forth, weeping uncontrollably for the first time since we met. You see, Nicole bragged that she was not very emotional and would probably not cry when we finally met. I had hit the softest spot in her heart, and now everything she had held back was flooding over her. She threw her glasses off, and I embraced her. At this point, Nicole and Aprile were both crying and were too emotional to continue reading the card.

I quickly put on my reader and read the card to them while they attempted to gather themselves.

To My Dearest Sisters Nicole and Aprile,
The Celtic Sisters Knot is a symbol of sisterhood and the strong, eternal bond we share with our sisters and friends.
I believe that the heart symbolizes our mother, Patricia Ann Franklin Blackston. It ties the three of us together from now on. I am so happy I have found you both. Thank you for embracing me into your lives and hearts. Please wear this Celtic Sister Knot necklace as a reminder of this very special day that we were finally united.
We will never let go of each other and I look forward to getting to know you better and sharing an unbreakable bond with you both! Due to the circumstances, we may not have grown up together, but it feels like we were never apart.
Remember... "Side by side or miles apart, sisters will always be connected by heart."
With Sisterly Love and Affection,
Gia Lana James

I presented them both gifts of our new unity. Two Celtic Sister Knot sterling silver necklaces along with a bracelet cuff that had the "Side by Side..." quote inscribed on the inside and "Gia ♥ Nicole ♥ Aprile" on the outside.

Previously, Aprile and Nikki shared with me that they both had matching sister tattoos and wanted me to consider getting one to symbolize our new union.

As I handed them their gifts, I jokingly said, "Here are your presents because I am not getting no damn tattoo!" The two continued to cry and laugh simultaneously, so I hugged them. It was such an emotionally charged moment that will forever hold a special place in my heart.

We continued to sit around and talk, and in walks Louis and Lawrence, who had our dinner of fried chicken, shrimp fried rice, and an assortment of drinks. We sat around and ate while continuing our conversations. After dinner, I handed Louis the gift I brought him. He received a card with the same front and picture collage as the sisters and he began reading my message.

To the Brothers I've Never Met, Louis and Derrick,
We have missed out on so much of each other's lives,
and my goal is to get to know you both.
I was blessed with an amazing adoptive family, and
I can't imagine my life without them. However, I
always wanted to know who I came from and who I
resembled. Throughout the years, curiosity took over
my mind sometimes and I was overwhelmed,
especially when I carried my first child. I would ask
myself how a mother could carry a child, give her
up, and never think of her again. Under the

circumstances, I now fully understand the selflessness, strength and sorrows that must have tormented our Mother all these years.

Now that I have found you, I am so thrilled! Getting to know our Mother through your eyes and getting to know you excites me so much. We will always be connected through our Mother, Patricia Ann Franklin Blackston. I believe her spirit was the force that led me to find you all.

Please accept this bracelet as a symbol of our interconnection and eternal bond. Wear it in good health and remember the day we were finally reunited. I am sure our Mom is smiling down on us and directed my steps to this reunion.

With Sisterly Love,

Gia Lana James

After he finished, he opened his gift box. It was a black leather bracelet with an intertwined knot in sterling silver on the top. I got up and put it on his wrist. He was so touched that he hugged me.

Now that the group was assembled, Tammie and Barbara had a presentation of their own to make. They made and presented us with beautiful, custom-designed royal purple t-shirts. In the center of the design was a pink heart with the name "Patricia" on it. Around the heart was a circle of five locking arms enclosing the heart, each in a different vibrant color. Each interlocking arm bore the names of all of the siblings in order of birth. We were touched and decided to wear the matching shirts to Louis' home on Saturday for a family barbeque in celebration.

Lovingly referred to as Poochie, Louis had built a new home in Slidell and was having a housewarming party. I expressed my desire to have all of us take a picture together wearing our new shirts.

Nicole's husband, Lavelis Sr., who would, under normal circumstances, have already retreated into the bedroom, surprised everyone, and stayed in the room, taking it all in. I was told that he was very close with Patricia and that so much attention was given to my visit, which seemed to interest him greatly, almost as if new life was breathed into him. Every once in a while, I looked over at him and winked to acknowledge that I was aware of his presence.

While we continued visiting and talking, Tammie asked Aprile if she could think back to an earlier time and recall something that tipped her off about her mother knowing about me. Aprile admitted that she did recall an instance. However, she had not told me because she was afraid that I would think Patricia thought negatively about me. I told her I would never believe that and wanted to hear the story.

"Ok, so, when I got Buster, I fell in love him because that was my first time having a dog," Aprile started. "My mama did not like animals, but when she came to our house, she tolerated Buster and would play with him."

Patricia would say, "I like how his little collar jingles."

Aprile continued to tell the story. "One day, I was on the phone with her and told her, oh Mama, I love Buster so much. I am so happy I have a dog. You need to get a dog."

Patricia replied, "Oh, I will get a little puppy, but I want a girl puppy and I'm going to call her Gigi. Her name will be Gia, but I am going to call her Gigi."

Aprile said, "Aw, that is cute, but you are not gonna get a dog."

Patricia replied, "I am going to get a puppy. I just want a baby to hold."

Aprile explained that they never thought of that moment before until they knew I existed. Now, the siblings believe it wasn't about the puppy for Mom, it was about getting back the baby she lost.

I said, "How would she even know my new name?"

Aprile said, "I don't know how she knew your name, but the type of mother she was, she would not have rested until she knew you were safe, and then she made peace with it afterward."

We discussed it further and concluded that maybe someone inside the adoption agency told her what my new name was because they saw this scared young girl making a tough decision to give her child up. Tammie believes she found out where I was and had eyes on me. She could follow me as long as I was still in New Orleans. Possibly, someone inside the agency knew under what circumstances this young mother had to give up her only child and felt sorry for her. How could the agency have information about the man who sired me, but it was omitted from my birth certificate? They knew his occupation and had a description of my father's mother.

I revealed that I had mistakenly thought Omar was my brother and that it was like a tale of two Patricia Anns as I told them the story and how it all unfolded. They were both born around the same year, died around the same age, and were both from New Orleans.

My sisters shared stories of our mother's culinary talents. I shared with them that was a trait that I must have inherited because I, too, loved to cook. I also shared with them that I knew how to prepare gumbo, shrimp etouffee, other items, and some of my favorite things to pick up while in the South, including pralines. They could not believe it because one of our mother's specialties was making pralines. They shared stories of how Patricia would eject everyone from the kitchen when she made pralines, the meticulous process she followed, and how they used to fight over who would lick the bowl. Our similarities were becoming very apparent.

This particular evening, as we were visiting, the subject of Patricia's husband came up, and I urged them to visit their father. Up until this time, they had not shared what they discovered about my adoption with him. They were happy about meeting me and wanted to share the good news with their friends, so I knew they needed to inform him before others did because that was not how they wanted him to find out.

I told them, "You never want anyone else to tell your story. You need to tell it." They quickly agreed and made it a point to visit him that next day.

Some of my sister's close friends came over to meet us, and we continued to put some pieces of the puzzle together through our conversation and shared theories about our mother into the night before returning to the hotel to get some rest to gear up for the next day's adventures.

"Adoption is not a birthmother's rejection but an unconditional love that inspires her to put herself last and do all she can for her baby." - Unknown

CHAPTER 19
CLOSURE

The next day, Nicole and Aprile ventured over to their father's house. They were worried about posting things on Facebook without informing him of my existence. They explained that he's been showing signs of dementia, and his children did not want the news to possibly aid in the decline in his health. Still, they weren't sure if he knew Patricia had another child before meeting him, and they did not want to taint his memory of his late wife.

Nicole and Aprile had a pleasant visit with their father, who had no idea that Patricia had had another child before their meeting, nor did she ever utter a word about it to him. His daughters shared details about the circumstances, showed him some pictures taken from the day before during our first meeting, and asked him if he wanted to meet me. He declined by saying that since his late wife never shared anything about me with him, he felt that I was there for them, not him and that he wanted them to enjoy me.

Meanwhile, during their visit with their father,

Tammie, Barbara, and I walked into the French Quarter in search of some breakfast. We ate at Cafe Beignet and enjoyed our meals. The place was buzzing with tourists, and the sporadic jazz music from small groups passing by added to the exuberant atmosphere. We even got a little boutique shopping in while waiting for Aprile and Nicole to tell us when we could fetch them after their meeting.

Once given the clear, I gathered my new family, and they arranged a meeting with our younger brother, Derrick. Aprile and her family were staying with him for the weeks she was visiting as she always did when visiting New Orleans, needing and wanting to spend time with him.

I already knew that Derrick was the brother who would be the toughest to come around to my camp. My sisters had already explained that he was incredibly close with his Mama and seemed lost without her. Patricia was his strongest ally, and with her absence, Derrick's world came off its axis. He was the person who I was the most nervous about meeting.

When I arrived, Derrick emerged from the house and walked towards me down the pathway. I greeted him with a smile.

Derrick asked when we embraced, "How are you doing, Ms. Gia?"

"I'm alright. It is nice to meet you."

He quickly replied, "You too."

Derrick looked into my face, shook his head, and said, "Yeah," as if he could tell in that moment that I was his sister. He knew from looking at me that I looked just like our mother.

We all went inside the house, got comfortable, and started to visit. Derrick's home was immaculate. He was a clean freak, but I learned he loved his family. There were framed pictures of friends and family all over the living room.

In the corner, leaning on the wall was a Saints framed jersey with a number one and the name PATRICIA on the back. The dedication read, "Patricia Blackston, Loving Wife and Devoted Mother of Four, April 27, 1949 - August 20, 2010." On the left was a beautiful headshot of her, and on the right was a letter from Derrick to his mother.

Another framed picture of a Navy uniform shirt with various medals and ribbons was awarded to Derrick. His service was significant as he set foot in Jamaica, Cuba, South America, Haiti, and Africa during his active duty. Other awards listed were the Navy/USMC Achievement Medal, National Defense Service Medal, Humanitarian Service Medal, and Expert Pistol Shot Medal. He was a very proud veteran.

Now, it was time for me to present Derrick with the card and gift I brought him. As I stood by him at the kitchen counter and told him I got him something, he looked at me, lowered his head, and said, "I am not worthy."

Something in his statement and stance caught me off guard, and I replied, "Derrick, I never want to hear you say that again! Just because we are from the same woman makes you worthy."

I then presented him with the same card I gave Louis and his own interconnection bracelet. He seemed so honored and proud to have me put it on his wrist, thanked me, and exclaimed, "It fits perfectly!"

Tammie made her presentation to Derrick with his personally created t-shirt. We continued to sit around, talk, share, and laugh. While we were there, Derrick gave us a tour of his body tattoos and what they all signified. I was so relieved that things went well that morning. Now, meeting all of my brothers and sisters was complete.

After leaving Derrick's home, my sisters and their families took Tammie, Barbara, and me to visit the site where my mother was laid to rest: Mt. Olivet Cemetery and Garden Mausoleum on Norman Mayer Boulevard in New Orleans. We visited a store along the way to purchase artificial flowers because Mt. Olivet did not allow us to place real flowers in the cemetery.

As we drove up, I realized she was resting in a mausoleum. I told everyone that we had that in common and that either being cremated or in a mausoleum was also my desire. Nicole asked me why I did not want to be buried, and I said I did not want to be under the ground where the bugs and worms could eat me.

Nicole just sat there, looked in amazement, and said, "Oh my God, that is the same thing Mama said!"

More proof: I was my mother's daughter and thought the same way she did.

It was a gorgeous, sunny day. As we walked toward the site, Aprile started to tear up, and I put my arm over her shoulder. She expressed that it had been two whole years since she visited her mother's grave and that it was still tough for her to believe she was gone. We continued onward as she was wiping away her tears. Nicole and Aprile pointed upward, and there was the marker, "Patricia Ann Blackston, Apr. 27, 1949 - Aug. 20, 2010."

"We're here, Mama," I announced upon our arrival, standing before her.

Aprile added, "Yep, we're here together."

"We got our big Sissy Poo. Yep!" Nicole chimed in.

We stood side by side, locked together, and looked up at her. I started having these inner thoughts of the finality of it all. I was now standing in this place at my mother's feet. A full-circle moment for me. Closure. I started tearing up while bringing my sisters closer to me.

Nicole explained that they laid her in row forty-nine because that was the year of her birth, and then there was a lot of silence and reflection.

The moment eventually came for me to place the flowers we brought. My niece, Makaylah, started to get emotional as her stepfather, Lawrence, comforted her. She was the oldest granddaughter and knew her grandmother the best.

Before I said a few words, I could feel the emotions welling up, so I couldn't speak for that long. I looked up, held the flowers, and said, "So I brought you flowers. It's too bad I could not bring them before you left. But I'm here now."

Once I placed them down, my sisters came to my side to comfort me. I wished I could have said more because this woman gave me life and protected me from evil, but I kept it simple. Patricia would know what was in my heart.

We continued to pose under her placard and take photographs with just my sisters and the whole family gathered. I wished I could touch the placard. However, it was too high. Tammie jokingly offered to hoist me up, but I just laughed, finding sweet joy in our solemn moment at that idea.

Then I reasoned aloud, "I guess this is the closest I will ever get to her."

Nicole replied, "Well, you were close at one point because you were inside her."

I agreed.

We all looked at the other graves nearby, including a section called Musicians Row, where many of New Orleans' great performers and musicians were laid to rest. The cemetery was very lovely and well-kept. My sisters told me about our mother's desire to be buried at Mt. Olivet, and she received her wish.

After leaving Mt. Olivet, we went to the Fiery Crab restaurant for a fantastic seafood boil. We shared more stories about Patricia, laughed, and continued to get to know each other better. Our server loved our story of finding each other after all these years. We returned to Nicole's home and enjoyed more time together before returning to our hotel for the evening. This was a good day.

The following week, after I shared the latest happenings via video clips and photos online, I received a late-night phone call from Julie, one of my sorority sisters. Julie called me crying after viewing the video from the cemetery, saying this was as close as I would get to my mother.

Julie said calmly but emotionally, "Gia, I am going to try to get through this."

She continued sharing that when her mother passed away, she visited her grave on a calm, windless, stagnant day. She prayed for a sign from God to reveal that her mother was still watching over her. At that moment, the wind blew hard. Julie felt the sign was her mother. Julie told me I needed to rewatch the video with what she just told me in mind.

Once I hung up, I went to my computer and found the referenced clip, and sure enough, as we stood there talking, and after Nicole said, "You were inside of her," the wind picked up at that very moment and blew both my dress and Aprile's shirt! Oh, my Lord! THAT WAS PATRICIA. She was trying to tell us that she was still there with us all. She was in the wind.

I immediately called my sisters and told them what Julie had discovered. They also rewatched it and texted me that they agreed. It was blowing our minds......in a good way! We just experienced a miracle.

Sometimes, it takes someone else from the outside to identify what you can't see. I am genuinely grateful to Julie for letting us know what she had witnessed.

"One day, you will understand why your timing was perfect. and why things had to happen exactly the way they did. To protect you, to guide you and to redirect you to where you were always meant to be. Trust the process of your path, evolution, and growth – It's all divine timing". - Unknown

---

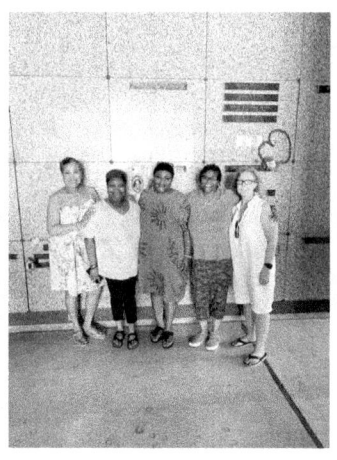

CHAPTER 20
THE FAMILY BARBECUE, FINGERS CROSSED

Saturday arrived, and it was time to venture out to Slidell to go to Louis' new home, sharing in family time. Louis had invited us all to come, including Derrick. I was hopeful Derrick would come, but he announced to Aprile that morning that he was not feeling well and would pass. Nonetheless, he sent, by way of his sister, a large bottle of Tito's vodka as a housewarming present to Louis. That was a grand gesture, and I was proud of Derrick for his acknowledgment of Louis and his new home.

On our way to Louis' house, I announced that I would bake a pound cake, so we needed to collect the ingredients. Nikki grabbed a Bundt pan and mixing bowl from her kitchen, as we predicted Louis would not have those items. While at Walmart, I gathered everything else, including my housewarming gift of a hand mixer. Everything was set, and we were off.

As we got closer to Louis' home, we decided to stop at TJ Maxx and do a little shopping for pleasure. I also went to the back of the store to retrieve some thank you cards so

Louis could write Derrick a thank you card for the Tito's. Once everyone was done shopping and made their purchases, we went to Louis'.

Louis welcomed us into his newly built, well-appointed four-bedroom ranch home. He had set up the grill in the backyard and was busily outside cooking. After we unloaded the car and were all settled, we began our kitchen duties.

Aprile was making chili for the hot dogs, and once the coast was clear, I began assembling things for my anticipated pound cake. Nicole, Aprile, and Louis described Patricia's pound cake as delicious with a little crunch on the bottom. I hoped I would not disappoint them.

As I was concentrating on the duties at hand, I noticed Aprile starting to photograph me as I was working. I looked at her, smiled, and continued to work... eggs, flour, sugar, extract, 7-up... Looking around again, I saw Aprile sitting at the table crying, and Tammie was comforting her. On approach, I asked, "What's wrong?!"

Tammie explained that as I put my ingredients together and started making the cake, Aprile was taken aback because she could only see her mother in the kitchen. I was doing things the same way our mother used to do, and Aprile was brought to tears while saying to Tammie, "I know the cake is going to taste the same as my mama's cake because Gia is making it the same way she used to do it."

All I could do was stop, hug her, and tell her everything would be okay.

Once the cake was in the oven, I set the timer, and we all started to eat the excellent food Louis had prepared... Hamburgers, hotdogs, hot sausages, ribs, chicken, salad and more. Everything was wonderful.

We had some great conversations while eating, and I

sat back with Louis and discussed his relationship with Derrick. I explained to him how he should approach their relationship from now on and that he could not "fix" Derrick or direct him to act and do something different. I recommended Louis be more patient with him and support Derrick instead of preaching to him. I also reiterated my desire to get a photo of the five of us together and asked when we could make that happen. He told me that Monday morning would work for his schedule, and he would be willing to come to New Orleans before going to work for the photo op. I told him I brought him some thank you cards and would like him to write Derrick a note for his housewarming present. He agreed to do it, and that was that.

My niece informed me that the cake timer was going off. The long-anticipated big reveal was almost ready. I took the cake out as everyone gathered around. The oohs and aahs were very audible. The cake had to cool a little before I could remove it from the pan and put the glaze on it. While waiting for that to occur, I decided to prepare the glaze.

Lana and Tuttie had watchful eyes on me and started to crowd around the counter. Therefore, I decided to teach them how to prepare the glaze. After ten minutes, I flipped the cake onto a plate and topped it with the glaze. The cake made its debut as everyone gathered around to take pictures of me and my siblings posing with the coveted cake.

I hoped the cake would completely cool before cutting it, but that did not happen. The pressure of needing to eat the hot cake was apparent as the ice cream emerged from the freezer. My siblings had first dibs on the taste testing.

The moment of truth had come. I passed a slice to my

sisters Nicole and Aprile, who tasted it, looked at each other, and said, "Mmmmm."

Louis reached over, secured his taste, and started dancing while chewing like a kid. "Ooh yeah, that's good. I need some ice cream!"

Aprile started dancing and exclaimed, "Tell Andy I'm moving in!"

"Oooh, Gia, that's good!" Nicole said in agreement.

Louis told me I needed to start shipping the cakes to them for the holidays. Nicole shared that it was nice and moist, but when she tried to go in for another taste off of Aprile's plate, Aprile shooed her away and said, "Uh uh, go get your own!"

Once the taste test was complete, everyone else swooped in for their slice and topped it with ice cream.

I interviewed my sisters and asked Nicole, "How did you like the cake?"

She replied, "The cake was wonderful. Nice and crunchy at the bottom. Very good. Reminded me of Mother. *Mmmmmmm*."

Next up was Lawrence. I asked, "Brother-in-law, how did you like the cake?"

Lawrence gestured, "Two thumbs up!"

Tuttie gave it a ten out of ten, followed by Lana, who gave it a twenty out of ten. Now for Aprile...

"This cake is *delicioso*!"

As he enjoyed another bite, Louis said, "Whew, this cake is so good. Gia, just leave me a piece for my late-night snack."

As Louis requested, I put his slices aside along with two additional slices for Derrick. Within fifteen minutes, there was no extra cake to be had.

Knowing I did not disappoint them was great, and they

loved it. We continued to enjoy each other's company. I taught my nephew and nieces how to play Quirkle at the kitchen table, and soon, on the back porch, the dominos were out, and family fun was afoot. As the night progressed, a few additional guests arrived. We laughed and talked until darkness fell.

Since we had a forty-minute drive back to the city, I could see that Louis had not written his thank you card to Derrick. Therefore, I retrieved them and pushed them toward him, requesting him to follow through with our discussion. I sat beside him and talked with one of his friends as he put pen to paper. When he was done, he pushed it toward me as if he wanted me to read, grade, and approve it. I put my hand over the card, turned to Louis, and told him that I did not need to read the card and that it was a private note to Derrick. I asked him if he meant everything he wrote in the card, to which he replied, "Absolutely."

"Good, then put it in the envelope, seal it, and I will give it to Aprile to deliver to Derrick."

With that being fulfilled, we gathered all our belongings and said our thank yous and goodbyes with another great day complete. Love and light were definitely in the air, and I was delighted, looking forward to our Sunday at church the following day.

Aprile left Louis' note on the counter with a note for Derrick to make sure he read it when he came home from his late-night job as a bouncer at a club. When Aprile arose the following day, the note had been retrieved.

Once Derrick woke up for the day, she asked him if he got the note. Derrick seemed as if he did not believe what Louis wrote, so he showed Aprile the card. It was basically a thank you card for the housewarming gift Derrick sent.

Louis told Derrick he was missed at the party and wished Derrick had come. Then he told Derrick he loved him and wanted to discuss things to repair their relationship.

I was so proud of Louis for writing this letter. At this point, both brothers were willing to come to an understanding after years of disagreement and not getting along. Time would tell.

That morning, Aprile and Derrick talked about my desire to have us all wear matching shirts and take a picture of five. Derrick agreed to do it on Monday, as Louis had said, and the decision was made to meet at Derrick's house around noon. My fingers were crossed.

CHAPTER 21
WHERE IS THERE?

The time had now come for me to experience what my sisters were discussing as it pertained to the church they faithfully belonged to. They love their Pastor, Jonathan Everett, who is the Pastor of "The fastest growing church not only in New Orleans but the WORLD!" or so they say at the start of every service. The Rock of Ages Church, located at 1921 N. Tonti Street in New Orleans, and is very small in stature, but large in numbers.

Nicole attends in person every Sunday, and Aprile is a dutiful "Bedside Baptist" while watching intently online from her Pine Bluff, Arkansas home. Nicole always says that you must get there by 8 AM for the 9:15 AM service so you can sit in the main part of the church. Otherwise, you will be relegated to the overflow section in the secondary back area of the building.

It was the first Sunday of the month, when everyone dresses in black and white. This dress code is requested by the congregation; my sisters made it mandatory for the family. So, we all showed up at eight at 8, bright and early, to share our new experience with my new family members and good friends, compliant in our best black and white. Since everyone showed up to be a part of the celebration, our family filled up two whole rows in the sanctuary. We were seated and in place as people arrived over the next hour to fill the church and overflow area.

Music filled the place as we waited, and the choir and band warmed up. My niece, Makaylah, sitting immediately to my left, leaned over to me and said, "Aunt Gia, please don't let it be too long before we see you again. You are the best thing that has happened to our family in a long time, and we must keep in touch."

Her request humbled me. "I won't, I promise." Makaylah's heartfelt plea touched me. It felt so good knowing that I made as much of an impact on them as they made on me.

As the time of the service drew nearer, my friend Tammie directed me to switch seats and sit between my sisters, so I heeded. As I got settled, Aprile reached into her purse, took out the most beautiful green Bible with pink flowers, handed it to me, and said, "I wanted to wait until today to give you this. Read it out loud."

On the main dedication page, it read:

Presented to
My Sissy Poo, Gia Lana James
(Shevonne Marie Franklin)
By Your Sissy Poo,
Aprile Catrelle Blackston Kenney
On June 4, 2023, in New Orleans, LA.

"Your word is a lamp to my feet and a light to my path."
- Psalm 119:105

I read her note aloud as my friends and family intently listened...

Dearest Sissy Poo Gia,

Every day since Mom passed away in 2010, I have prayed so much that God would send a piece of Mom back to us because I have missed her so much. Words could not ever explain, and I would feel like God was not listening to me and Mom was just gone and so far away, and there was no sign of her, but I never stopped praying. In this process, her death has moved me closer to God, and I'm grateful for that, even in the pain and sorrow of her being gone. But when I thought God was done with me, he sent us you!!! I cannot tell you in words how much you mean to me and how much you have done in my life since we met. I realize now that Mom was gone physically, but she was very much still watching and mending our hearts from above. I don't feel like we have missed a beat even though we didn't grow up together. It feels like we were never apart, even though we were miles away.

I'm happy to say now that you were what I prayed for, and God has finally answered my prayers because he sent us you. So I want you to take this little bible as a token of my love to you, and every time you pick it up and read it, it reminds you that even at our darkest times and even when we think that God isn't listening to us, He is always with us, even if he is silent. I love you, Gia, and I'm so excited to take this life journey together called sisterhood. I hope that this strengthens our prayer life even more together.

I can do all things through Christ, who gives me strength. Whatever I have, wherever I am, I can make it through anything in the one who makes me who I am.
- Philippians 4:13

I began sobbing before I could finish reading Aprile's note. Aprile moved close to me and embraced me tightly. I was overcome with emotion as I started to digest what finding my family meant to me and how timely it was for them as well. This was the beginning of a healing of sorts for the whole family. And most importantly, for our mother, Patricia.

The choir ramped up to begin the service. After the announcements and hymn selections, Pastor Everett arrived at the pulpit and started his lesson for the day, reading from 1 Kings 17:4 (King James Version).

"And it shall be that thou shall drink of the brook, and I have commanded the ravens to feed thee *there*."

Pastor Everett explained that this is the first time that a different class of birds is publicly referred to in the bible. They usually are just referred to as birds, but in this case, the ravens, the worst and lowest class of birds, were referred to illustrate that the lowest class will be called forth and made to obey Him, God.

He then read the second verse, 1 Kings 17:9.

"Arise, get thee to Zarephath, which belongeth to

Zidon, and dwell *there*: behold, I have commanded a widow woman *there* to sustain thee."

The pastor asked the congregation to emphasize the word *there* each time. He continued and said he wanted to preach a sermon today called "*A Place Called There.*"

Pastor Everett started by saying that as we continue to walk with the Lord, situations always reveal who God is, who God was, and who God is going to be. This walk with the Lord is not primarily for you to become a better version of yourself. Christianity is not about you bragging about who you are, what you have, and where you go. When Christians start using their liberties and materialism to try to describe how blessed they are, you discover they are not as blessed as they say they are. It says that what they have has *them*—true blessings from the Lord, Jesus Christ. In fact, some of the *greatest* miracles were done in private.

Whenever people broadcast in public how anointed they are, by how loud they speak in tongues, it doesn't tell you they are anointed. It tells you they want some attention. Anyone who is driven by rage and loudness lacks the peace of God. The peace of God teaches you how to talk when to speak, where to talk, who to talk to, and what to talk about.

When someone who calls themselves a Believer shows you they are willing to argue with everybody and anyone, they suggest that they have no intellectual standards. You should not argue over opinions but only over the actual authoritative figure of the Lord, Jesus Christ. When walking with God, you will see some things that baffle you because God does things incrementally but never incompletely.

When God shows up for you in your life, it is beyond you; it is not for you but for somebody else around you. God is not only a God of Power but also a God of Principle.

Principles are rules of operation for a thing that comes from the creator of that thing and ensures preservation, protection, and productivity. Anything unutilized is because the person has not come into the fullness of their identity. God, of Principle, knows what you need and when you need it to be the best version of who He wants you to be. You don't take a Mercedes Benz to a Honda dealer to be repaired because they aren't the maker of the Mercedes to ensure long-lived preservation.

Don't ask everyone else about you; ask the Creator since He knows what is best for you. We must strive to be more productive physically and spiritually with the time we have here on Earth. Be productive because you live by principles. Principles are the direction God sends us to give us what He promises. We pray for peace and relationships, amongst other desires, but prayer alone does not enhance your relationship with God. If you want to enjoy the fullness of God, you need to follow His principles! Faith without works is dead.

Isaiah 26:3 states, *"You will keep in perfect peace, him whose mind is steadfast because he trusts in you."* Sometimes, your mind is elsewhere, but when it is time for the blessing, you are the first in line. You can't receive a blessing you did not pray for. You are not petitioning God for His favor when you are not applying His principles.

I realized that this Sunday's lesson spoke to me in a way I could have not have imagined. I had quietly and privately prayed to God for His assistance in finding the answers I was seeking all this time. I kept the faith and persevered through it all, never giving up. I have been seeking the fullness of my identity for over twenty-five years, and now my prayers have been answered.

Thank you, Lord, for leading me to my place called

THERE! There's healing *THERE*. There's deliverance *THERE*, there's power *THERE*, Your anointing is *THERE*. I tried to force you to rearrange the timing of it all. This season, I was hungry for where *THERE* was; that was where I wanted to be.

You may not have come through when I wanted you to, but you did come through right on time! I should not ever question *Your* timing. This was the ordained order and time for me to find out the answers that you had for me. You put me in the right place at the exact right time. THERE looks different from what I thought it would look like. Some hidden figures protected me while I was weary while searching for the answers. You took care of me along my journey and never failed me.

My nature mother, Patricia, was trying to unselfishly protect me by giving me away instead of letting the hands of those who harmed her bring that same harm to me. She was trying to find out where THERE was, and you helped her by guiding her steps to take me to the Children's Bureau of New Orleans. I was blessed with my new adoptive family that nurtured and raised me THERE. Finally, in coming full circle, I am now THERE and can see the fullness and difference in my life that finding my siblings and their families has brought me.

I sat in that place, flanked by my two precious sisters. These realizations came forward and revealed themselves to me. I was overwhelmed and began to weep tears of joy. Aprile leaned over, put her arm around my shoulder, and whispered, "Gia, you are *THERE*."

I was *FINALLY THERE*! I was home, and nothing could bring this feeling down.

As church ended, there was chaos because Pastor

Everett needed to depart to guest speak at another church. He was in the back after the service because my niece, Lana, had prepared a gift, a painting of the church to present to the Pastor for the 100th anniversary that would be celebrated soon. This Pastor always makes time for his congregation, so he thoughtfully allowed for the presentation. My sisters quickly took me up to the side of the church's altar because they knew the Pastor would exit from the church to his car that way.

As he emerged from the church's office on his pathway to exit, Nicole reached out to him and said, "Pastor Everett, this is my new sister. The one that I told you about. I wanted you to meet her."

The Pastor stopped and greeted me by shaking my hand and smiling. He said, "It is a pleasure to meet you. What do you have to say?"

I paused, humbled myself, and replied, "I am *THERE*."

He stepped back, looked at me in amazement, and said, "Wow!"

I do not think he knew until that moment how his sermon impacted me. We quickly went to the front of the altar, where he motioned to his escorts that he would be right behind them in a moment and let my family take a picture of me with him to commemorate that moment before he exited the church. I was full.

My family all congregated to take group photos before departing Rock of Ages Church to spend the rest of our day together. We shared a family meal at Mr. Ed's Oyster Bar and Fish House, followed by seeing *The Little Mermaid*, starring Halle Bailey as Ariel. It was another memorable day indeed.

"Let us not become weary in doing good, for at the proper time, we will reap a harvest if we do not give up." - Galatians 6:9

CHAPTER 22
THE PICTURE OF FIVE

We only had a few days left to continue bonding as a new family, so I was beginning to think about the beautiful memories we made and what we had left to do. Lawrence and Makaylah had to leave early that morning to return home due to Makaylah's work schedule, so we said our goodbyes the previous evening. This marked the first of my goodbyes to my new family, and I already dreaded the end of our fabulous week together. Today was the day for us to finally don our customized shirts and take a picture of all five of us together. I started to worry... Will Derrick back out? Would Louis show up? Would they have words between them, and then the whole thing would turn into something negative? Shaking myself to keep from these thoughts, I started thinking more positively and prayed to God to let this day go as planned.

We arrived at Derrick's house at 9:30 am and were all visiting in the family room. Aprile announced that Derrick was in a foul mood, and after the picture was taken, she was ready to leave so we could have fun together. I called

Louis to make sure he was on his way over. He confirmed he was not that far away and would arrive by 10:00. Derrick was still in his room, getting ready with the door closed. I approached his bedroom door and knocked ever so lightly so as not to startle him.

He immediately shouted, agitatedly, "Can I at least get some God-damned clothes on!"

From this, I realized that he must have thought I was Aprile, so I replied pleasantly, "Sure thing," and walked back into the family room, taking my seat. He really did wake up on the wrong side of the bed. Now I could see what Aprile was dealing with.

Due to some health issues, Derrick seems to not feel well sometimes, but he has a sweet and quiet nature while I was around him. Once he finally emerged from his room wearing his matching shirt, I felt a sense of relief that he was still open to carrying out the picture of five. I jumped up, hugged him, and said, "Good morning, brother! Thank you so much for agreeing to take the picture today even though you are not feeling well."

He was immediately calm after our exchange.

I'm unsure if he felt calm towards me because I reminded him so much of our mother or his unfamiliarity with me dared him to give me a little attitude. He would have died if he knew it was me that he cursed out on the other side of his door only a few moments ago.

Louis arrived on time, and we all started gathering on the front lawn for the photo op. As the two brothers approached each other, they shook hands, said hello, and embraced. Tammie dutifully photographed this monumental moment. These two had not said a kind word to each other for a while, and we were all hoping this would be a pivotal moment in their relationship. In my head, I could hear the angels singing Hallelujah.

The five of us lined up according to birth order, and Tammie quickly did her job as photographer and documentarian. We took several photos with different poses until we were satisfied that we had memorialized the big event.

Nicole and Aprile shared with me during an earlier conversation that they were not even sure the family album included a picture of the four of them together. Finally, achieving this picture of five made me feel so accomplished that my goal had been reached. This was proof that all five of us were siblings, and we were finally united as one unit, completing the previously fractured circle around our mother, Patricia. I was in a state of euphoria, but I felt there was one more item to attend to.

Now was my opportunity to bring my two brothers together and speak with them. I pulled each of their hands toward me so they faced one another. As I looked up, the others were intently watching. I asked them if I could have a moment with my brothers. Suddenly, as if someone turned the lights on, and the cockroaches scurried away with such a quickness that they were all spooked by what was about to happen. Once everyone moved out, I spoke to Louis and Derrick.

I told my brothers that there was a reason why I came into their lives at this particular moment in time. I believed that our mother ordained my steps and led me to them. Patricia knew they needed me, and I needed them, too. She could not come, so she sent *me* in her stead. I told them that they did not have to be the best of friends, but they needed to be civil to one another and have a relationship that allowed them to speak with civility and maintain a brotherly bond. They most likely did not even remember why they were angry with each other, but now was the time for both of them to try.

I confided that my relationship with my adopted brother was estranged, and I vowed to both of them that I would take inspiration from their situation to extend an olive branch to him. I would only ask them to do what I was willing to do. Derrick and Louis immediately started vocalizing that they had no problem with each other or my request. They would begin to communicate and take the necessary steps towards reconciliation. They shook hands and embraced one last time as Louis got in his car to leave for work.

Woo hoo! The picture of five was etched in stone, and things looked up for the day. Now, we were en route to meet my cousin, Stephanie, who had such an impact on connecting the dots so we could experience the riches of this week.

The Picture of Five

Monday Restaurant and Bar was located in a residential area in the Mid-City section of New Orleans. The place was buzzing with patrons. I would finally meet Stephanie in person, and now she would also meet my sisters and friends. How would I recognize her? As we approached the courtyard, I noticed a beautiful, dark brown-skinned, small-framed woman sitting on a bench covered by an umbrella. I knew this was Stephanie.

I walked right up, greeted her, and hugged her. After introducing her to my friends and family, we started sharing how our relationship had manifested and how we have been joined at the hip since the previous summer. Stephanie explained that she also thought she was related to my sisters on both sides of our family.

We were seated in the outdoor patio section of the very hip restaurant. We enjoyed the conversation and started to decide what we wanted to order from the diverse menu. After we ordered our meals, I handed Stephanie the gift I brought and requested that she open it immediately. She first opened the card and started reading the outside of the card. It read, "Not All Heroes Wear Capes." As Stephanie opened the card and saw the same collage I put inside my siblings' cards, she gasped and stared at it while tears started welling up in her eyes, saying, "Oooh, Gia. That's beautiful."

As I requested that she read the card, Stephanie said, "Oh, Gia, don't make me cry. Do I have to read it out loud?"

I replied, "Yes."

"Damn!" Stephanie exclaimed.

"We all want to cry," Nicole added.

Then Stephanie started to read aloud.

Dear Stephanie,

Having you be an instrumental part of this journey has been such a blessing. Thank you for being a part of my story and for everything you did to show me that you have my back. Going through the process has been scary at times, but knowing you were behind me every step of the way and were a HUGE part of solving the puzzle made everything a little easier. Please know that I appreciate you and all of the time and efforts you made on my behalf to reunite me with my siblings and find the answers we were looking for. You will always hold a special place in my heart. You are my hero! Plus, I got a bonus cousin out of the deal....YOU!

Please wear this infinity bracelet in the best of health as a symbol of my eternal gratefulness to you. We must continue to keep in touch.

Love, Gia

Stephanie started tearing up as she finished reading the note. She thanked me and said, "There are so many hurting people in this world because of the secrets that people hold, and this has been my most satisfying victory. Even though my family and I are still estranged, I am feeding off of you guys. Thank you. You know I love you."

She then reached over and gave my knee a soft swat.

I replied, "You know I love you too, girl!"

Stephanie opened the box, and I had the honor of placing the bracelet I selected for her on her right wrist, which fit perfectly.

Lunch arrived at the table, and we continued to visit while enjoying our meals, which consisted of fried catfish, crawfish etouffee, fried oysters, and the pièce de résistance, sweet potato beignets, which Tammie and Barbara loved.

I was so glad we could have this much-needed time with Stephanie. We talked about a trip to Aruba together, so I packed that in my memory bank to plan something soon. Lunch was such a wonderful part of the day. We hugged and kissed as we parted ways until we would see each other the next time.

We dropped Barbara off at the hotel so she could put her feet up. Her ankles had swollen from the heat and all of our walking. Barbara also knew that the time had come for us to let Tammie get her shop on and visit every TJ Maxx store in New Orleans! It was not her scene, so we put her out of harm's way.

We were locked and loaded on a mission to grant Tammie's wish. It was me, Tammie, Nikki, Aprile, and Lana, and we were off to the races for the remainder of the afternoon, ducking in and out of each TJ Maxx and coming out with our treasures. We loved being in each other's company and laughed until tears started falling. We knew we were now inseparable and dreaded the end of our incredible week together.

Later that evening, when we were all in bed, I received a text from Aprile informing me that she did not feel well. We all assumed it must be from something she ate. Louis was planning to come from Slidell to take us all out to dinner for our last night in New Orleans, and we hoped Aprile would feel better in the morning.

Nikki wanted us to meet us in the morning at the drugstore she managed because she wanted all the people she worked with to finally meet me. She had taken the entire week off to be with all of us, and this was the only morning left to go to the store.

We met Nikki at the drugstore where Aprile was purchasing a test to determine if she had COVID. She was wearing a mask to protect everyone, just in case. In the meantime, we met all of Nikki's work family as they all crowded around to finally meet the person who had caused the commotion in Nikki's life. They were so friendly and welcoming.

We thought it best for Aprile to go home and take her test immediately, so Tammie, Barbara, and I returned to our hotel to await the call. I received a FaceTime call within the hour. Aprile had the most sad look on her face and said, "The test was positive. I have COVID." She turned her camera around so we could view the results for ourselves.

Oh my Lord, Aprile felt so horrible that we could not spend our last day together, and it looked like she was ready to start crying. I comforted her by saying it was ok and it wasn't meant to be. The good thing is we were able to make all these beautiful memories for the whole week. She agreed, but you could tell the lowness in her spirit.

Nikki said Louis was coming to pick us all up for dinner. After thinking about it, we had all been exposed to Aprile, and we thought it best if we called off the dinner, so I hung up, called Louis, gave him the bad news, and asked him to turn around and go home. There's no need to expose him, too. *DAMN*! This was a shame.

Little did I know I would not see my sisters again after the store visit. *UGH*. Tammie, Barbara, and I packed our suitcases in the hotel room. Barbara decided to change her flight and leave that evening instead of the next day because of the new developments. We decided to FaceTime the Sissy Poos throughout the day in place of our planned togetherness. It was the next best thing.

While lying around, I told Tammie and Barbara, "Hmmm, I think my throat hurts."

We started laughing, thinking because we knew Aprile was sick, our minds were playing tricks on us, and we were inventing symptoms somehow.

The following morning, Tammie and I packed up the van with our belongings and ventured to our final rendezvous at Cafe Beignet for breakfast before heading to the airport to return the rental car. I had a fleeting thought of doing drive-bys with Aprile and Nicole. However, Nicole was not home as she had to take her husband to a doctor's visit. I did not want to do it for one and not the other, so we just left for the airport.

My throat worsened, and I thought I was coming down with a cold.

When I got home on Wednesday evening, I immediately took an at-home COVID test. It was negative. Whew, maybe I had dodged a bullet. Tammie reported a negative test as well. I followed up on Thursday morning with another test, which was negative, but my throat was still achy. Friday morning, I took another test. *POSITIVE! OMG.* I went to my local urgent care center to have them administer a PCR to confirm and started to isolate in my basement bedroom just in case so as not to expose my family. Thank God my mother-in-law was still in Baltimore.

Result... We all got COVID-19: Aprile, Nicole, Tammie, me, and eventually Lana. Barbara must have escaped it because she did not go on the TJ Maxx shopping spree! However, we continued daily FaceTimes and told each other we would do it all again, including getting COVID-19, because the trip was memorable, so much fun, and well worth it all.

"Your journey has molded you for your greater good, and it was exactly what it needed to be. Don't think you've lost time. There is no short-cutting to life. It took each and every situation you have encountered to bring you to the now. And now is right on time." - Asha Tyson

---

CHAPTER 23

REFLECTIONS

My journey has been long and tedious, but it was gratifying. My story has a happy ending, but I will tell anyone walking in my footsteps that even though your story may not have an ending like mine, you have every right to know your truth. Don't fear what you may find in seeking the answers you need to feel whole or validated.

Knowing my truth has set me free in a way I never dreamed of. Finally, getting nuggets of health history really answered some of the questions I needed to know about what happened in my life before this, and it helped me to understand what things I need to look out for going forward. Having siblings to share things with and walk alongside, especially the closeness with my sisters and my relative's acceptance, both biological and adoptive, has deeply touched me in my soul. It is a feeling of belonging, calm, and deep-rooted love that is difficult to describe, and I most likely will never find the words to do so.

I used to ponder what it would have been like if I had been able to find my biological family earlier and had the opportunity to meet my birth mother. I can finally say that the experience would not have been as sweet as how it unfolded. Patricia decided to put me up for adoption and never reveal to her husband and children that she had given birth to me. This was a secret she and her father, my grandfather, chose to keep. They made a pact, and they stayed true to their word. Had I come into their lives while they were still alive, that would have disrupted their world, and my four siblings may have protected her and shunned me. They would have had to take sides and make a choice, and I know they would have stood by their mother.

It took losing her, missing her, and longing to have her back after thirteen years for them to open their hearts and get a piece of her back in the form of me. It is still eerie to them how much I look and act like her. Things like how I pick at and eat my food, how I cut my eyes and facial expressions, and the fact that I say "samich" instead of sandwich that we are still discovering through our daily FaceTime calls and visits that amaze them. They call me "Little Pat" sometimes when I freak them out or say things that remind them of her.

Similar name coincidences like how I came to know my given name at birth, how I always wanted to name my first daughter Siobhan, and how my niece, Lana, has my middle name kept happening as well. One of my beauty technicians is named Shavon, and one day. I went to tip her through an app after our session together. When I received a thank you message from her, the email that notified me of her message said, you have a message from Shavon Marie! You know, that gave me chills. No way! HER NAME IS SHAVON MARIE TOO! What are the chances that Shavon Marie is doing services for Shevonne Marie? It is not a typical name combo. These are messages from above signaling me everything is happening in divine order, and I am where I am supposed to be.

Our fate was meant to play out this way so we could fully rejoice in experiencing one another. As for my brothers, Derrick and Louis....A calm seems to wash over Derrick when I am in his presence. He was very close to Patricia and missed her dearly. He tends to stare at me when I am around like he is looking at her through me, which comforts him. I look forward to getting to know him better and forming a bond with him, as he is more reserved than Louis. Louis calls me weekly to see how I am doing and is excited about seeing me again. Meeting his children, who reside in Dallas, is a mission of mine in 2024. Louis is charming and very accepting. The next time I go to Louisiana, I plan to spend some time with him and stay in his new home in Slidell. I also want to spend a few nights at Derrick's and spend time with him and my sisters.

Each Sunday, while visiting my birthplace, New Orleans, I plan to worship with the Rock of Ages Baptist Church with Pastor Jonathan Everett. Pastor Everett's sermon, A Place Called THERE, was the message prescribed for the congregation on that specific Sunday. I attended the services with my newfound family and girlfriends and, as you now know, the inspiration for the name of my memoir. While not in NOLA, attending weekly services virtually with my sister Aprile and watching for Nicole in the audience as the camera pans out has been the highlight of my Sundays. After service, our daily Sissy Poo FaceTime call completes my day and sets the tone in my spirit.

Thanksgiving is coming closer and closer, and the high anticipation of our two families finally meeting in person for the first time is quickly approaching. Jazmyne and Jordyne already have plans for late-night talks in the slumber party den I set up in the basement, going for cheesesteaks at Delassandro's in Philly, running up the Rocky Steps at the Philadelphia Museum of Art, family game night, and movie-watching in the man cave. I am excited for my sisters to visit my home and finally meet my family, especially my mother, Myrtle, and my dog, Teddy.

We talk all the time about the menu we will prepare during the week of their visit, comprising of fried turkey, lasagna, oxtails, red beans and rice, mac and cheese, pound cake, red velvet cake, and sweet potato pie, to name some items. We plan to have an open house so my friends can meet my new expanded immediate family. I look forward to having most of my loved ones under one roof for the first time.

Looking back and reflecting on my very colorful life, I have learned that every experience, obstacle, and challenge I have faced was placed there for a reason and has taught me a lesson, building me up into the resilient yet stubborn, forthright, and boss lady I have become. Every experience, negative and positive, has had a hand in forming who I am. I am the Gia today because of everything that occurred. This version of Gia is loved, worthy, and deserves to be happy.

I would also like to pause to acknowledge and sincerely thank my mother, Myrtle, who raised me with love and gave me opportunities I may not have gotten if raised by anyone else. She instilled in me a sticktoitiveness and work ethic that I cherish greatly. The childhood memories from growing up with her and my family have made a lasting impression on me, and I cherish and love her and my family.

Moving forward, spending time with my true friends and family is now my first and foremost mission in my life.

My priorities are more apparent, and I see my goals in color now. Creating new adventures with my entire family is a goal, and being a new channel of life experiences with my siblings is so important to me. Letting go of undeserving distractions, finding balance, and putting myself first is a new focus of mine. Making myself happy and almost being selfish in doing so is something I am no longer afraid to do. This experience has inspired my 58-year-old self to live freely and passionately and love myself and others unconditionally.

"Embrace uncertainty. Some of the most beautiful chapters in our lives won't have a title until much later." - Bob Goff

---

EPILOGUE

Hello again...Since the release of my book happened after Thanksgiving 2023, I wanted to give everyone a synopsis of what occurred so as not to leave you all hanging.

Thanksgiving was beyond wonderful as everyone had an opportunity to meet and enjoy the new meshing of family. Aprile and Nicole loved getting to know my mother, Myrtle, and vice versa. My sisters have dubbed her "Mama Myrtle."

We ate all that we planned to, including the coveted Philly cheesesteaks. Andy selected a night to go down to the basement and deejay for us as we all danced the night away and played pool. My daughters enjoyed the atmosphere as well and meeting their new aunties. Jordyne brought her boyfriend, Dalen, home, and he enthusiastically shared in the fun of family game night. We laughed uncontrollably until we cried at times. This Thanksgiving was truly unforgettable and will leave a lasting impression on everyone.

My sisters have created an aunt and niece group chat to

continue their relationships over the miles, which is working well.

Our Sissy Poo slumber parties each night in the basement were wonderful, and it gave me and my sisters the precious time we needed to continue to bond further. Of course, we were dreading being separated again. Still, we looked forward to our next rendezvous in January when I would travel to Pine Bluff, Arkansas, to celebrate my niece Lana's 18th birthday on the 10th and then go to New Orleans to celebrate Nicole's birthday on the 16th with Teddy in tow.

The day after Thanksgiving, we finally had our professional photoshoot in our home, followed by an open house where about 50 people came to meet my sisters. Warmth and laughter were present, making my sisters feel like movie stars. It was so wonderful for them to know that my circle truly cared about their existence and presence in my life that will radiate into the world. We are forever changed for the better.

The best is yet to come as we leave for Aruba in June 2024 for our sister/friend's trip. Although we can't change the past, we move forward with a vengeance filled with love, happiness, and hope.

MY LOVE NOTE TO SHEVONNE MARIE FRANKLIN

Dearest Shevonne Marie Franklin,

You may not know it from the beginning, but you will be so richly blessed and loved by countless people in your life. Your nature mother, Patricia Ann Franklin Blackston, unselfishly put your needs above her own desires and protected you from harm's way by placing you safely in the arms of another mother, your nurture mother, Myrtle Ball Garrison, to raise and love you as her own. Although Patricia longed for you all her life, she knew that this was in your best interest. The bond between you and your mother, Patricia, is so unknowingly strong that even though you were apart, you could still hear her whispering your birth name in your ear, and even in death, she is always swirling around you in the wind, constantly protecting you from evil.

Through your life's journey, you will encounter many people who will play a significant role in your life, especially your adoptive family and hosts of good, close friends. Some people will be put into your life to teach you lessons, good and bad. They will mold you into the strong-willed, stubborn, yet loving person you will become. There will be stumbles and snares that you will encounter, but you will persevere through it all and finally come to a place of understanding who you are. ***You will discover your Place Called THERE.*** You will finally be at peace and will reap the benefits of all the joy that the Lord has for you.

Live well, play hard, be happy, and love yourself unapologetically.

Love,
    Gia Lana Garrison James

BONUS

Thank you for joining me on this extraordinary journey.
Please enjoy these reflections from my family, highlighted
by a heartfelt letter from my mother, Myrtle, in memory of
my biological mother, Patricia.

Family photos and two recipes are also included.

A REFLECTION FROM DR. MILDRED BRIGHT

MY AUNT

As I look back on my life with Gia, pure joy comes over me, and a smile comes to my face. It's a true blessing to be a part of this unique life experience.

My first meeting with Gia was when she was a small child in her mother's arms. I was so excited to see my twin sister Myrtle and her children as they arrived in Houston from New Orleans by car with my husband, Gia's Uncle Billy. My sister said to me. "This is Gia. This is my golden nugget". And, of course, she immediately became my golden nugget because that was my twin sister, and what was hers was mine. Our life has remained that way.

Of course, I could never call her that because that's what her mother called her, and I gave her my own name, which was Gigi. Over the years, I have so many wonderful memories and some challenges that we have lived through.

Gia has always been direct. She has been the person that told you exactly what she thought regardless of the price she had to pay. You knew where she stood. If she agreed to do something for you, you could count on it being done. On the other hand, you could negotiate with her. If she changed her mind, she would work hard on the project. This became a problem with some adults when Gia was a child, but Gia knew how to stick to her position. When she felt she was right, she would tell you so.

If you really want to have fun, watch Gia and her cousins! They have so many stories to tell about each other as children together. Two of my favorite stories are Gia at the Sand Dunes with her cousins and Gia beating the ice Zamboni machine on the ice-skating rink when she was afraid that it was coming.

I love you, Gia.

-Aunt Mildred

A REFLECTION FROM JAZMYNE JAMES

MY OLDEST DAUGHTER

Dear Mom,

I can recall overhearing you discussing your trying to find out more about your family history since I was in my teens. At the time, I didn't fully understand what this meant.

You and Dad always made a point to introduce your close friends as family members, so for a while, I naively thought that everyone introduced as family was actually related to us. Obviously, as I grew older, I came to understand and appreciate the definition and value of a "chosen" family and an adopted family.

Like you, I was always curious about the possibility of your finding your biological family, but I felt that it wasn't my journey to embark on. Witnessing you figure out where you came from and the first heartbreak you experienced after establishing a connection with a man you thought was your brother saddened me. It was a disappointment that I had not seen on your face, and I thought that this would be the end of your journey.

Much to my relief, you stuck with it, and that's when

the excitement returned to our lives. Now as an adult and being back home, I felt honored that you involved me more in the mystery of your origin. Being a participant and first-hand witness to the evolving story of you was never something I thought I would be privileged to experience. From finding out about your cousin, Stephanie, who was a Genealogist, to her taking the reins and placing the puzzle pieces together like an expert detective was truly something to behold. Then the day came when you both found it, the final piece, your biological mother!

I can recall us sharing a drink as you shared the series of events of how you came to be and the possibility of finding your newly discovered siblings. You were nervous to reach out, but I knew how important it was to you and to no surprise, it did not take much encouragement for you to make first contact.

After the ice was broken, watching you and Nicole build a connection felt both beautiful and eerie. It was nice to see you forming a sisterly connection, but I was also apprehensive because of the speed. I felt conflicted telling you about my anxieties when you shared that you would be going to New Orleans to meet everyone in person. I was reminded of some of the talks you gave me growing up about how to always keep an eye out on people, even though they can seem familiar quickly. I also expressed that my main concern was seeing you hurt or disappointed once again. However, I was reassured knowing that Auntie Barbara and Tammie would be joining you. My worries severely dissipated seeing the joy and relief in your eyes upon your return.

As I write this, I can remember all the times we, as a family, would make jokes about your "witchy" powers with premonition and how they can be used for good and "bad."

I am convinced that they are real. I'm sure that your readers will be, too, once they read about the details we have been experiencing as a family and your story. Jordyne and I are convinced that they are genetic, but those are other stories to tell.

In conclusion, I want to take this moment to just say how blessed I am to have you as a mother. Even through times where I didn't understand what your thoughts or reactions were, you have always been there to love and support me. Now, as a grown woman, I cherish the times that you and I talk about life and share with me your stories and experiences that are sometimes shockingly similar to mine. You have always been a light that shines bright with everyone you meet. I'm positive that it will radiate even brighter once we get together this Thanksgiving. You always say this to me, so now this is one of my opportunities that I get to say this to you...Mom, I am so proud of you, for not giving up, and for always seeing things through not only to the end, but open to new beginnings. I love you!

Your Daughter,
Jazmyne

A REFLECTION FROM JORDYNE JAMES

MY YOUNGEST DAUGHTER

If you have made it this far in the book, then you have learned a lot about my mom. You probably have a good sense of her strength, compassion, perseverance, and humor. What these pages will never be able to capture is her extraordinary spirit. My mom does not simply light up a room; she sets it on fire. Her energy is powerful, radiant, and warm. She has the wildest and most infectious laugh, the best style, and the silliest slogans. My mom is the most gregarious person I know, finding endless ways to support others. She is the last to go to sleep because she can't stand going to bed without a spotless kitchen or because she is finishing up tasks for her sorority. She refuses to put her cell phone on silent just in case somebody needs her. I swear she never misses a phone call. Her ringtone from 15 years ago still haunts my sister and I. When I was in college, I called her at 3 AM to ask for the Netflix password. My friends doubted that she would answer, but I had not a single doubt in my mind. Of course, she answered, followed by a "Really, Jordyne?" She still proceeded to find the password for me. My mom goes above and beyond for everybody she loves, which is why am so proud that she finally dedicated time to invest in herself.

My mom has pursued many passions throughout her life, and she has somehow succeeded in all of them. When I was young, she decided to switch careers and become a real estate agent. She quickly became an award-winning agent in our town in New Jersey. I was so proud of my mom's job. All I wanted was to be just like her. I remember being as young as eight, and her taking me to her open houses and letting me pretend to give tours to her clients. A few years ago, she decided to aid in developing a local Alpha Kappa Alpha Sorority (AKA) graduate chapter. Within four years the chapter was up and running, she became the president, and she went on to hold a regional position. Being that my sister and I were grown and out of the house, I would say AKA has been my mom's biggest passion over the past 12 years. That was until earlier this year when she decided to continue a journey she began long ago. This time, it changed our lives forever.

From the very beginning of the process, I saw a completely different side of my mom. My mom is usually very optimistic, but since this was not her first time trying to find her birth family, I could tell she was both hopeful and reticent. I decided that my role was to hold all the optimism for her and encourage her through the process with the same confidence she always has when encouraging me. I will never forget my mother's reactions to opening her original birth certificate, seeing her DNA match results trickle in, reaching out to her birth sister, and meeting her family in person. She has gone through a lifetime of emotions. The proudest I have been of my mom was witnessing how she reacted when her birth sister initially rejected her outreach. My mom instantly respected her birth sister's feelings, shoving aside her own disappointment and lifelong desires. Again, always putting others above herself. She was too strong to show how disappointed and heartbroken she was at that moment, but I knew. After a lifetime of build-up, she was finally there, and in one instant, it all came crashing down. It took everything in me to hide my upset in that moment. I had to be strong for my mom, but I also understood how unfathomable it must have felt for her sister. Luckily, my auntie ultimately came around and, as you have read, the rest was history.

Mom, I am forever blessed and proud to be your daughter. We both know I was certainly not an easy kid to raise. I have been giving you a run for your money since the moment I was born. Leave it to me to get stuck in the birth canal during delivery. One thing is for sure, I get my most difficult traits from you: spunk and stubborn determination. In a similar vein, the greatest lessons you have taught me are resilience and perseverance. You have not taught me by telling. You have taught me by being. You are the most incredible woman I will ever know. I look forward to gaining more pieces of you through the family you have finally discovered. While your journey to find your roots is complete, so much of your story is just beginning. I will be there for you, as you have always been there for me every step of the way. I am so very proud of you, Mom. I love you infinitely.

To my newfound family, thank you for opening your hearts. I know it has been a whirlwind, but I am so glad it was worth it.

With Eternal Gratitude and Love,
Jordyne James

A REFLECTION FROM APRILE BLACKSTON KENNEY

MY SISTER

Where do I start? First of all... I want to start by giving praise and honor to my Lord Jesus Christ because without him this journey called life wouldn't be possible.

I am the youngest of all my siblings. I grew up with two brothers and one sister. My life, I guess you could say, was like many other people. We didn't have much, but our parents always gave us the best. We didn't want for anything. My father was a hard worker, and my mother was a homemaker, so she was always there when we needed her. My mom and I were very close, and we shared a lot of things. I always thought that I knew everything about her. My childhood was a good one. I had friends, went to private school, and I had everything that I desired. My mom was the backbone of my family she kept everything together for us in her good and bad days.

Fast forward to 2010. That is the year that I lost a part of me that could never be replaced. I lost my mom, Patricia Ann, that day I will never forget, and it's the hardest thing I have ever been through in life thus far. Even though the pain was unreal I was grateful that we had a close relationship and we were open with each other. So, I had no regrets, and I felt as if nothing was left unsaid.

I was wrong because it turns out there was another part of Mom that we never knew. Life certainly has a lot of surprises, and we got the biggest surprise on Facebook Messenger one day in the form of Gia James saying she was our half-sister that our mom gave birth to her at a young age. When we heard this, we immediately thought she was crazy because there was no way our mom had another child and never told us anything, so we thought.

I guess this proves to me that you really don't know everything about someone. When we learned that this is in fact true and Gia was our sister indeed I had so many emotions from happiness to sadness because mom was no longer here to meet her but I know she had something to do with us coming together again from up above.

Meeting Gia has been the best thing that has happened to me besides the birth of my children and marrying my husband, that is. It has really been amazing having her in my life, learning about each other, and finding out that we have so much in common, and all of the coincidences are just freaky...LOL, like the fact that her middle name is Lana. When I learned this, I was blown away because that is also my daughter's name. It's just pronounced differently. Also, I learned that she was the owner of a breed of dog called Shelties. They are a smaller version of a Collie, and presently, I am a dog mom to a Collie named Nola. We both love to cook, we both are housewives, and we have so many similarities. It's crazy!

I never imagined that this would be happening to me. I always thought we were a family of four kids, and all the while, it's been five of us, but I will say that having her has been such a blessing. She has come into our lives, and she fits right in. There was never an uncomfortable feeling; it just feels like we grew up together our entire lives. She is just like mom, she looks like her, acts like her and she is bossy too just like her, but I love it because I feel like in a way I have gotten a piece of mama back and now that we have her we will never let our precious Sissy Poo go.

Sincerely,
Sissy Poo Aprile Kenney

A Reflection from Nicole Blackston-Fountain

MY SISTER

Since Gia has come into my life I have felt as though I had my mother back. Also, I never knew what it was like to have a big sister. She gives me that motherly big sister advice. She has helped me see some things from a different perspective. She has shown me unconditional love, and I'm very comfortable with her. I will do just about anything for her, and I'm sure she feels the same about me.

I love having an older sister, especially someone who reminds me so much of our mother, Patricia. She has the same exact mannerisms as our mom. Especially the bossiness and her caring for other people. She even cooks like her. The genes are very strong. It just goes to show that it doesn't matter if she didn't grow up with us; genetics do not lie. Even though when the news of Gia's existence came about at a time when I was going through a very stressful time and our relationship did not look like it was going to turn into what it has.

I'm over the moon about Gia. I'm loving the direction our relationship is going and through our relationship, I have inherited a whole other family. So, I'm looking forward to meeting everyone and continuing on this joyful journey that we're on. I'm also excited about the relationship she's developing with my son, at first he was kind of shy around her, but now they have their own little relationship. It's still developing, but it's happening. I love to hear her stories from when she was growing up. Some things are really eerie to hear because even though we didn't know each other before now we are basically just alike. So I said all that to say even though the circumstances were not ideal around her conception, we don't harp on that. We just concluded that we got something great out of a bad situation. I love my bossy GiGi and I wouldn't change a thing.

-Sissy Poo Nicole Blackston-Fountain

A LETTER FROM MYRTLE BALL GARRISON

TO PATRICIA ANN BLACKSTON

Dearest Patricia,

As I look back in wonder and before more time passes, I want to let you know of my deep appreciation, privilege and pleasure it has been to have received and raised Shevonne Marie Franklin, our adorable 3-month-old baby daughter. For appreciation never depreciates. She was placed with my family of three by a private closed legal adoption agency in New Orleans, Louisiana, in 1965.

I strongly believe that "family is where life begins and love never ends." As I've contemplated your particular courageous circumstance, let me say here that without you, there would not be me. "For who takes the child by the hand, takes the mother by the heart." - Danish Proverb

After such a daunting and perplexing situation that you endured, the unplanned experience of young motherhood, I can only imagine the anxiety, trepidation and complex emotions that you encountered as you carefully considered your options and future life. I also know that it took great courage, along with anguishing moments, to place your baby for adoption. Perhaps there were times when you thought you had made a bad decision. But, even in the middle of your most serious doubts, ambivalence and deepest fears, you probably always wondered whether your unerring decision was the best for both you and your baby and what would be her fate.

We were not apprised of any information about Gia's biological family, nor their health history. At an early appropriate age, I told both my children that they were adopted, which they accepted favorably. I often wondered if Gia's cute features, radiant smile and sparkling brown eyes resembled yours. Additionally, I wondered if there were any pertinent negative inherent genetic familial health history concerns. Notwithstanding those unknowns, I immediately loved and bonded with our beautiful daughter when she was first placed in my arms. Many years later, during Gia's search for you, she sent me your photo. I could readily observe Gia's resemblance to you; your facial contour, eyes and beautiful features.

Gia's health history became most important during her pregnancies. It was at that point that she decided to search for her family.

As I can recall Gia's stages of development through childhood, she was healthy, without allergies, happy and an observant baby. In anticipation of Gia's arrival, she shared the bedroom with her two-and-a-half-year-old brother. Her baby bed was placed adjacent to his colorful bunk beds. The room decor and circus-themed bedroom, red and white bed skirts and curtains were uniquely designed by me. During my two-week parental leave from work, Gia was a happy, contented, alert baby who bonded with me and made an easy transition into her new family.

She adapted to her immediate surroundings, as Gia's brother happily entertained and interacted with her during her waking hours. They loved playing together.

We purchased a second home where Gia now had her own bedroom. When Gia was about nine months old, she was active, sociable, and gregarious. She met all the developmental milestones before or near the target ages. I can vividly recall her first head lift, radiant smile, rolling over, crawling, pulling up and standing inside her crib and the eruption of her first tooth. She was insatiably curious and as she progressed, she asked "why" a lot. She was given appropriate answers by me. At an earlier time, Gia's only latex pacifier was always readily available which kept her oral sucking needs satiated, especially when she slept. Quite often, it fell from her bed when she needed it late at night, those unfortunate infrequent incidents resulted in her high-pitched screams. From my deep sleep, I immediately heard her cry and retrieved the well-worn pacifier for her.

As a working mother whose employment duties entailed providing anesthesia services during the weekday and responding to emergencies, this demanding work schedule made the consistent enrollment of childcare a necessity. She adjusted quite well to all the daycares, made friends easily, was well-liked and enjoyed those experiences. During preschool, she developed good social skills and encouraged some shy and isolated children to enjoy group interaction and play. At the age of 3, she loved to have bedtime stories read from the *My Bookhouse* library. She was unwearied, independent, easily adaptable, personable, honest, and kind. She learned such skills as swimming and jumped off the diving board. She approached other lessons and activities, such as piano, ice skating, tennis, and gymnastics, with enthusiasm.

Today, Gia's core family of four is a deeply-rooted tree with branches of different strengths, all receiving nourishment from an infinite source. One of the highlights of Gia's life was her wedding in Houston, Texas. As the mother of the bride, one of the proudest moments of my life was to escort Gia down the aisle and present her hand in marriage to her wonderful husband of now 35 years. Their family is "a haven of rest, a sanctuary of peace, and most of all, a harbor of love."

As I view Gia's adult life, she is an amazing, compelling composite of inherited qualities received from her natural mother integrated with those cherished, cultivated, and nurtured supportive qualities, all bound with abundant, endless love and affection from her adoptive mother.

Gia, our adult daughter, is now a well-rounded, genuine, light-hearted, devoted wife, mother, daughter, true friend, a good neighbor, and citizen who has traveled extensively on the road of life with many turns which have brought her to this very special time and place where she has finally met her biological siblings. Although you are not actually at this family meeting, she strongly believes you were there in spirit, courageously watching over her.

Now I am sensing that your previous tears of fear have been alleviated and your tears of joy have prevailed. You have shown that "life's inevitable adversities call forth our courage." If you could only know the phenomenal woman she has become you would be justly proud.

Now that Gia's years of searching, yearning, and longing to know her birth mother and biological family have finally and happily become a reality, she has achieved her indispensable goal. With bountiful love, Gia has now reconnected the broken Franklin family chain. Gia's story ended well. "For all is well that ends well." - Shakespeare

With deepest gratitude and affection,
Myrtle Ball Garrison

Patricia Ann Blackston

Gia's Pound Cake

SERVINGS: 12   PREPPING TIME: 15 MIN   COOKING TIME: 1 HR 15 MINS

Ingredients

- 3 sticks butter
- 3 cups sugar
- 5 whole eggs
- 1 teaspoon butter extract
- 2 teaspoons vanilla extract
- 3 cups all purpose flour
- 1 cup Sprite or 7 Up

Glaze:

- 1 cup confectioners sugar
- 1 tablespoon Whole Milk, or as needed for consistency
- 1 tsp vanilla extract

Directions

1. Preheat oven to 350 degrees.
2. Cream butter and sugar together.
3. Add eggs one at a time, mixing after each addition.
4. Add butter and vanilla extracts and mix well.
5. Add flour, one cup at a time, mixing well after each addition.
6. Add Sprite or 7 Up, them mix together until well combined.
7. Pour into prepared Bundt Pan and back for 1 hour and 15 minutes until the tester comes out clean.
8. Remove the cake from the pan after 20 minutes and cool while making the glaze.
9. Into a small bowl add the confectioners sugar, milk, and vanilla extract. Whisk to combine. Evenly drizzle the glaze down the sides of the cake before serving. ENJOY!

PATRICIA'S RED BEANS AND RICE

A Louisiana Tradition!

SERVINGS: 4   PREPPING TIME: OVERNIGHT   COOKING TIME: 2-4 HRS

INGREDIENTS

- 1 lbs. Camellia Red Beans
- 1 large yellow onion, chopped
- 2 tbsp. minced garlic
- 1 cup vegetable oil
- capful of Zatarain's liquid crab boil
- Creole seasoning to taste
- 2 pig tails
- 2 bay leaves
- 1 ½ - 2 lbs smoked sausage cut into coins
- hot prepared white rice

DIRECTIONS

1. Sort beans, cover with water and soak overnight. In the morning, drain and rinse beans.
2. Put whole pig tails in a separate pot and boil for about an hour to get the salt out. Drain that water and set the pig tails aside for later.
3. Add soaked beans to a dutch oven, cover with new water.
4. Add chopped onions, bay leaves, oil, crab boil, a little creole seasoning and garlic. Cover and bring to boil over medium/high heat. Once it reaches a boil, turn down the heat to slow cook, stirring occasionally for 2 to 2½ hours until they start to "cream". If the beans do not cream, you can take a spoon and mash some beans on the side of the pot. Note: Add more water if necessary, but be careful to not add too much because you do not want your mixture to be too thin.
5. Add pig tails and smoked sausage and continue to simmer for 1½ to 2 hours. Stir often to avoid sticking at pot bottom.
6. Taste and add more Creole seasoning if necessary.
7. Serve over hot parboiled white rice and enjoy!

NOTES

Camellia brand red beans are a staple of this dish. Other brands do not "cream" as well. This recipe can be doubled depending on the amount of people you are serving.

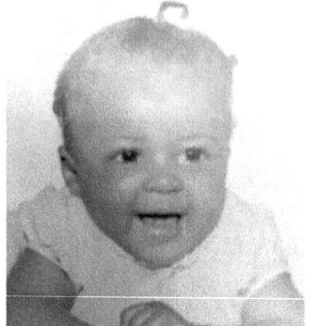

Gia around 5 months old

Gia around 6 years old, 1st grade

The James Gang

Gia and Andy in 1989, 1 year married

Jazmyne James, age 31

Jordyne James, age 28

My dog, Teddy!

Myrtle Garrison, Gia's Adoptive Mother

Gia with Pastor Jonathan Everett,
Rock of Ages Baptist Church

Barbara, Gia and Tammie

Jordyne and Jazmyne (top)
My family/friends at church (left)

Photoshoot pictures at Thanksgiving, 2023

Front of greeting card to siblings

Sisters, Aprile, Gia and Nicole
(l to r)

Brother Louis and Gia

Gia and Brother Derrick

Acknowledgments

- Andrew James... for being my partner in life, provider and loving me with all my quirks and imperfections.
- Jazmyne and Jordyne James, my beautiful treasures and daughters. I am so proud of the intelligent, strong, beautiful, and great women you are blossoming into.
- Myrtle Ball Garrison - for adopting me, raising me, loving me, and lifting me up always with your infinite support and wisdom.
- Dr. Mildred Ball Bright, my aunt, second mother, and a constant source of encouragement. You knew I could, and so I did.
- My cousins, Stephanie Martin, Audrey Franklin Bean, and Farien Franklin Christian, thank you for helping me put the puzzle pieces together and figure out where I fit in your lives.
- Tammie Cottom and Barbara Fleming: *Sweet friendships refresh the soul and awaken our hearts with joy, for good friends are like the anointing oil that yields the fragrant incense of God's presence.* - Proverbs 27:9. I can't thank you both enough for carrying me and being my girlfriends.
- My biological siblings, Louis "Poochie" Blackston, Jr., Nicole Renee Blackston-Fountain, Derrick Blackston, and Aprile Catrelle Blackston

Kenney, for embracing me into your family and making me feel welcomed and loved. For believing my truth even though you were blindsided with all of it. I hope this book will help introduce me to you all. It can't make up for the years we weren't connected, but this is our new beginning. Get ready and hold on for all kinds of crazy that we will go through together. We have a lot of time to make up.

- To "Omar": You played the role of brother for ten whole years before God saw fit for me to find out my reality. Even though it was not what we originally thought, you will always be considered my family and will hold a special place in my heart.

- My sorority sisters in love, You know who you all are, and you are too many to name.... who listened to me and cried with me as I walked through all my emotions, screams of discovery, and tears throughout my journey.

- To my entire sorority and ladies of Alpha Kappa Alpha Sorority, Incorporated, who prayed for me and stood behind me in support and camaraderie.

- One of my oldest and dearest friends, Monet C. Davis, for being there for me and being genuinely you.

- Some of my other sisters in love, Deborah James and Alberta Crescenzo, for being there for me to confide in throughout the years.

- Pastor Jonathan Everett and the Rock of Ages Baptist Church in New Orleans, Louisiana, thank you for helping me to reflect on my spirituality and many blessings and bring God's word to me every Sunday since June 4, 2023!

- Richard Wah of Wah Photography and John E. Bowser, Jr., for taking beautiful shots of my family in our home the day after Thanksgiving, 2023. The way you captured our family was second to none. Thank you for helping to capture such an important and special time in our lives.
- To my hairstylist, Valerie Lambert, who keeps my crown on point and has listened to me drone on and on about my life challenges and hash through my feelings.
- To Len "Cruze" Webb of The Bat Base for all your coaching and assistance in facilitating the recording of the audiobook version of my memoir. You coaxed me out of my comfort zone, but it was well worth it.
- My publicist and friend, Keisha Mennefee of Honey Magnolia, thank you for assisting me through the steps of telling my story and getting it out there to the readers. Your excitement surrounding my truth was heartwarming, and you made me feel truly special and supported.
- Finally, thank you to my biological mother, the late Patricia Ann Franklin Blackston, for making the ultimate sacrifice but also giving me life and being my constant guardian angel in the wind and in Heaven.

ABOUT THE AUTHOR

Born in New Orleans and raised in Houston, Gia's journey through life has been rich with experiences that shaped her into a fervent advocate for adoptees and a voice for personal discovery. She holds a degree from Carnegie Mellon University and has enjoyed a diverse career before committing to author her memoir.

Gia is also an active member of Alpha Kappa Alpha Sorority, Inc., through which she engages in community service and leadership. In her personal time, Gia loves to explore the culinary traditions of her New Orleans roots and experiment with new recipes, often infusing her dishes with a taste of her heritage. Her commitment to family, community, and her sorority exemplifies her dedication to uplifting others and celebrating the strength of familial bonds.

She is the proud mother of two daughters, Jazmyne and Jordyne, who are the light of her life. Gia, her husband Andy, and their beloved dog Teddy happily reside outside of Philadelphia, Pennsylvania.

www.ingramcontent.com/pod-product-compliance
Lightning Source LLC
Chambersburg PA
CBHW071154130626
46553CB00004B/1648

* 9 7 9 8 9 9 0 7 8 1 7 0 2 *